THE BASIC BOOKS

OF

RUDOLF STEINER

THE BASIC BOOKS
OF
RUDOLF STEINER

A Compact Guide for Personal and Group Study

RICK SPAULDING

WRIGHTWOOD PRESS

ANN ARBOR

Copyright © 2018 by Rick Spaulding
All rights reserved.

Wrightwood Press
www.wrightwoodpress.org

The cover illustration of Ginkgo biloba is a detail of a book plate from *Flora Japonica, Sectio Prima (Tafelband)* by Philipp Franz von Siebold and Joseph Gerhard Zuccarini, 1870.

Edited by Maurice York.
Book design by Maurice York.

NON-PROFITS, LIBRARIES, EDUCATIONAL INSTITUTIONS,
WORKSHOP SPONSORS, STUDY GROUPS, ETC.
Special discounts and bulk purchases are available.
Please email sales@wrightwoodpress.org for more information.

August 2018
ISBN   978-0-9801190-7-7

To Peter Demay — a true study group leader, a mentor, and a spirit guide on the anthroposophical path

Charts

Chart I ♦ 10
Theosophy Chapter one — The Essential Nature of the Human Being
(Carl Unger's Chart)

Chart II ♦ 11
Theosophy Chapter two — Destiny and the Reincarnation of the Spirit
(Carl Unger's Chart)

Chart III ♦ 13
Comparison of the Spiritual World in Theosophy and in Occult Science
(Hans Gebert's Chart)

Chart IV ♦ 24
Knowledge of Higher Worlds Chapter 6

Chart V ♦ 34
Relation of Occult Science to the Basic Books of the Eastern Path

Chart VI ♦ 52
The Philosophy of Freedom Part I

Chart VII ♦ 55
The Philosophy of Freedom Part II

Chart VIII ♦ 58
The Basic Books (1902 — 1909)

Chart IX ♦ 79
World Literature

Chart X ♦ 90
The Renewal of the Arts (1909 — 1916)

Chart XI ♦ 117
The Social Initiatives (1916 — 1923) and The Founding of the General
Anthroposophical Society (1923-25)

Contents

PART I: THE BASIC BOOKS AND THE FIRST PERIOD OF
THE ANTHROPOSOPHICAL MOVEMENT (1902 - 1909)

    The Dawn of the Age of Light and the First Three Basic Books   3

    The Relation of the Basic Books to the Mystery Streams   32

    The Philosophy of Freedom   44

PART II: THE RENEWAL OF THE ARTS AND THE SECOND PERIOD OF
THE ANTHROPOSOPHICAL MOVEMENT (1909 - 1916)

    The Northern Mystery Stream and the Activity of Anthroposophia   59

    The Heralds of the Michael Age in World Literature   68

    The Mystery Dramas and the Renewal of the Arts   78

PART III: THE SOCIAL INITIATIVES AND THE THIRD PERIOD OF
THE ANTHROPOSOPHICAL MOVEMENT (1916-1923) AND
THE FOUNDING OF THE GENERAL ANTHROPOSOPHICAL SOCIETY
(1923-1925)

    The Threefold Social Order and the Opportunity for Social Renewal   91

    The Impulse of Freedom Founded in the Social Initiatives   96

    Steiner's Core Mission and the Founding of the General Anthroposophical Society   107

APPENDIX

THE FOUNDATION STONE MEDITATION   120
    by Rudolf Steiner – *A new translation*

ENDNOTES   124

PART I:
THE BASIC BOOKS AND THE FIRST PERIOD OF THE ANTHROPOSOPHICAL MOVEMENT

1902 – 1909

THE DAWN OF THE AGE OF LIGHT AND THE FIRST THREE BASIC BOOKS

THE BASIC BOOKS OF RUDOLF STEINER PRESENT a pathway from the earthly realm to the higher worlds. *Knowledge of the Higher Worlds* begins with the thought that "there slumber in every human being faculties by means of which he can acquire for himself a knowledge of higher worlds."[1] Human beings need to awaken and take up the task of reaching the next higher stage of spiritual development. People need to attain the state of imaginative consciousness that will characterize the next cultural age in mankind's evolution. Steiner called the age that preceded the present one the Greco-Roman epoch. We now live in the age of freedom. The spiritual beings upholding our world have withdrawn from our sight, and their seeming absence has permitted the possibility of freedom to arise for most human beings. Able to take his or her own direction in hand, each individual is faced with the choice of whether to reunite with the spiritual guidance previously available to all mankind.

In the past such guidance could be found in religious institutions and in the so-called mystery centers. In accord with the advice of a priest or the efficacy of an occult ritual, a human being could, hopefully, be pointed in the direction of the good. As a free person, however, such guidance pales before the voice of one's own conscience. For Steiner the appearance of the Reformation signaled the end of the classical age and the entrance into the modern age of freedom. The basic books written by Steiner were an effort to provide for the thinking life of modern man what conscience had brought to the moral life.

Steiner intended each of the basic books for the general public, writing more than one to better present the many paths to the higher worlds. Each book was an effort to harmonize with the freedom of the reader. Although he presumed a certain degree of literacy, Steiner made a concerted attempt to avoid jargon and intellectual abstractions. He provided a full and detailed explanation of each step on the path of initiation, along with numerous warnings and reminders. More importantly, Steiner outlined the

The First Period: 1902 - 1909

effects of the exercises of meditation and concentration so that the student knows exactly what is expected and what may be the result. Anyone thinking that the next stage of mankind's development will come about naturally is in for a rude awakening. In accord with the ideal of freedom, Steiner insisted that a full picture of the path, along with all of its pitfalls and effects, be supplied to the student before he or she could freely choose to take up the path.

A basic book has two primary characteristics. It is written for the general public, and it contains a complete path—a bridge, as it were, to the higher worlds. Only in its form as a book can it fulfill its most important task of preserving and honoring the freedom of mankind in the present age. It can be studied or not, be put on a shelf, or carried into one's life. A book is simply not the same as a guru, nor does it require physical exercises like yoga. Such guidance and exercises may have been beneficial in the past, but they cannot substitute in the present age for the ego's own activity and the development of one's own thinking. It is unfortunate that a book can be misread, but anyone with good will can make the effort to reread or even to take notes. The reality is that a basic book does not tell the reader what *must* be done and in what order, but what *can* be done. A free human being must preserve his or her freedom by deciding what to do and why.

With the founding of the German Section of the Theosophical Society in October 1902, Rudolf Steiner took on a leadership role, but at the same time he continued giving courses at the workers' school and two other associations, as well as touring cities in Germany and throughout Europe to lecture on various topics. In the summer of the following year, he founded a magazine and wrote articles for it of interest to the membership. In 1904 he began writing the basic books, which appeared in serial form in his magazine. Membership began to grow, and by the following year there were nearly four hundred members in eighteen different locations. Four years later the membership had almost quadrupled. A love for the spiritual world and a deep dissatisfaction with the experience of a profound emptiness in nature and in daily life drove this remarkable increase. The publication of the basic books further encouraged members in their belief that a path to higher worlds did indeed exist, and that reading such books could enable them to achieve their goal.

The First Period: 1902 - 1909

At the same time, Steiner created a complementary aid to taking up the path of initiation in the form of the study group. Forming a group of like-minded people and meeting at a regular time and place to converse with them about such books enabled a kind of active thinking to arise that is essential to advancing further on the path. Steiner's problem was that between his writing and lecturing he lacked the time needed to lead a study group. The person that he chose to take on this responsibility was Carl Unger. His role as study group leader was primarily to exemplify active thinking. The two main difficulties Unger faced were the tendency of some participants to recount personal recollections that the spiritual thoughts had triggered in them, and the habit of others to relate these spiritual ideas to modern science and its intellectual theories. Unger developed a way to avoid such problems by having a participant read a paragraph aloud and then try to put it into his or her own words, in a single sentence if possible. This method of digesting spiritual science and recreating its central meaning anew is the key aspect of active thinking. A group leader emulating Unger's method can assist the participants in building up living thoughts and elaborating them into a thought organism. Steiner said the experience that occurs when a group conversation develops properly can be called "being lifted out of oneself."

The tendency of participants in a study group to challenge the validity of the ideas of spiritual science can make the task of the group leader difficult. The goal of open-mindedness must be kept clearly before the group. Blind faith in such ideas because they came from Rudolf Steiner is harmful, but intellectual objections that can be raised against spiritual ideas and personal experiences that can be adduced for or against the truthfulness of them are superfluous. The question is whether such an idea can be taken in by each individual and held as a possibility so that its truthfulness can reveal itself in the life experiences of the coming years. Insofar as one's common sense comes to approve of a spiritual thought over time and the thought itself comes alive and begins to unfold, its truth will abide. The experience of active thinking is ever the touchstone of the success of conversations in a study group.

Leading study groups allowed Carl Unger to attain a deep and comprehensive grasp of the first basic book taken up by the members of the German Section. Unger published the results of his research in

The First Period: 1902 - 1909

Notes on Theosophy.[2] In simplest terms, his method was to reverse the manner in which Steiner had written *Theosophy*. Since Steiner had used a topical outline to compose the chapters in his book, Unger wrote out summary sentences for each of the paragraphs in the various chapters. He took these summaries one step further and even developed a chart or diagram for each of the chapters. Chapter one, "The Essential Nature of the Human Being," coalesced into a chart of the nine-fold being of man. The three rows showed the tripartite nature of man beginning with the body and ascending to the soul and then the spirit. The three columns reflected the threefold conditions of form within each row. From right to left, the physical form comes first, then the etheric, and finally the astral.

Though it resembles the childhood game of tic-tac-toe in its simplicity, Unger's diagram is permeated with meaning. Moving from the first row to the second, which shows the tripartite nature of the human soul, can illuminate the ordeals of soul that constitute the lesser mysteries. Moving to the top row creates a reversal, since the spiritual members are arranged from left to right, and opens insight into the higher stages of knowledge. Like a mantra this diagram

CHART I

*Theosophy Chapter one —
The Essential Nature of the Human Being
(Carl Unger's Chart)*

Manes (Spirit Self)	Buddhi (Life Spirit)	Atma (Spirit Man)	SPIRIT
Consciousness Soul	Mind Soul	Sentient Soul	SOUL
Soul Body	Etheric Body	Physical Body	BODY
ASTRAL	ETHERIC	PHYSICAL	

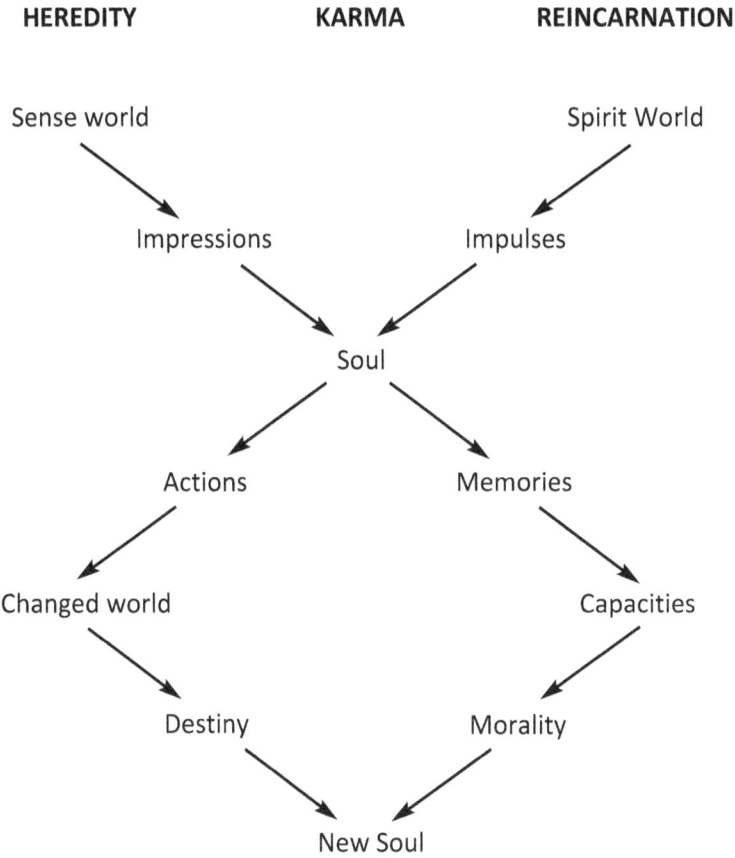

will reveal further insights the more often it is taken up as an object for meditation. Steiner believed that no one, himself included, would outgrow the basic books: "Better to read one lecture fifty times than fifty lectures once."

Unger also provided a diagram for the second chapter of *Theosophy*, given above.

Steiner faced a challenge when writing *Theosophy* in that he had to use the terminology of the Theosophical Society. In its attempt to gain perception of the soul and spirit worlds, this Society had followed an Eastern path. Rather than making this path more accessible to the European and Anglo-American members, the Society's leaders tended to preserve the Eastern terminology. This influence can be seen in Unger's first chart, where Sanskrit words are used to name the three highest members of man's essential being. In the first edition of *Theosophy*, Steiner tried to help Westerners by including his own translations in parentheses. Chapter three presented a more difficult obstacle—the description of the spiritual world itself—, which Steiner only surmounted five years later with the publication of *Occult Science: An Outline*. For instance, the lowest region of the soul world is called *Kama loca* in the Sanskrit language, which

CHART III

*Comparison of the Spiritual World
in* Theosophy *and in* Occult Science
(Hans Gebert's Chart)

THEOSOPHY   **OCCULT SCIENCE**

COUNTRY OF SPIRIT BEINGS	Christian Terms	Planets	Spiritual Scientific Terms
Spirit Self	Seraphim	(Zodiac)	Spirits of Love
Human Creativity	Cherubim		Spirits of Harmony
Archtypes of Soul	Thrones	(Saturn)	Spirits of Will
Archetypes of life	Kyriotetes	(Jupiter)	Spirits of Wisdom
Archetypes of minerals	Dynamis	(Mars)	Spirits of Movement
SOUL WORLD			
Soul life	Exusiai	(Sun)	Spirits of Form
Soul force	Archai	(Venus)	Spirits of Personality
Soul light	Archangels	(Mercury)	Spirits of Fire
Likes and Dislikes	Angels	(Moon)	Spirits of Twilight
Wish substaniality Mobile sensitivity Burning desire		(Earth)	

Steiner translated as the "place of burning desire" in *Theosophy*. Demonstrating this inherent linguistic difficulty, Hans Gebert gave a lecture in October 1981 in which he showed the transformation of oriental wisdom through medieval Christian esotericism to modern western spiritual science.

The student can grasp the path of knowledge presented in chapter four of *Theosophy* by summarizing the paragraphs in the manner that Carl Unger recommended. The first four paragraphs are introductory and orient the student to the idea that living thoughts are seeds; that all spirit knowledge lies dormant within the human soul; that living thinking promotes physical and mental health; and that spiritual thoughts need to be awakened and recognized as such. The middle section contains six exercises: learning from the world; becoming tolerant toward people; having pleasure and pain become the eyes of the soul; thinking logically without being distracted by the will-o-wisps; gaining full control of one's actions; and maintaining calm during life's challenges. The concluding paragraphs point to the need to develop a true estimate of each thing we experience, along with a will to freedom and a freedom from doubt.

The First Period: 1902 - 1909

The student can best understand the six exercises that constitute the heart of chapter four of *Theosophy* by turning to the basic book that immediately followed it. In the same year that he published *Theosophy*, Steiner began writing articles that appeared in the magazine for members of the German Section and other interested subscribers. These essays became the eleven chapters of *Knowledge of Higher Worlds*. Published at the end of 1904, it too belonged to the Eastern path. The task of this new work was to develop a proper terminology for the stages of higher knowledge, the different realms of the soul and spirit worlds, and the spiritual beings that inhabit them. This basic book differed from the earlier one in that the entire text was devoted to exercises of concentration and meditation. Whereas esoteric groups generally restrict their own members' access to such knowledge, Steiner explicitly and consciously wanted to present the truths of spiritual science in the same fashion as would a mathematics teacher. A math teacher would not ask a student to accept the idea that the sum of the angles of a triangle equals 180 degrees simply on authority.

Steiner's decision to reveal esoteric truths that had remained hidden under an oath of secrecy for millennia was not greeted with great happiness. While some secret societies had made an effort in the latter half of the nineteenth century to counter the rising tide of materialism by conducting séances and supporting spiritualism, most of them had decided to maintain their strict prohibitions against making their secret knowledge public. Steiner himself believed that a spiritual event had occurred at the end of the nineteenth century as momentous as the Renaissance and the Reformation, which had heralded the end of the Greco-Roman age. The modern era of freedom left the Age of Darkness and entered into the Age of Light in 1899. The Kali Yuga, which the Greeks had called the Iron Age, came to an end. The doors of heaven began to open, as it were, and spirit light began to shine for modern mankind. Steiner believed that this occult truth lay behind the Great War, and maintained that World War I and the calamities that would follow were actually the result of certain secret brotherhoods misusing their occult powers for selfish reasons and political gain. He indicated that the "eighth day" (as Thornton Wilder would later call it) required initiates to selflessly make public the knowledge that had formerly been hidden.

The First Period: 1902 - 1909

Steiner believed that free human beings, if given access to esoteric knowledge, were more than capable of finding real solutions to the problems of modern life and society. He emphasized the importance of taking up meditation as part of this process. Neither a guru nor any other kind of spiritual leader was necessary—simply a full explanation of the various exercises and their physical, mental, and spiritual effects. Yet Steiner did warn that study groups taking up the content of *Knowledge of Higher Worlds* should not engage in discussion of personal experiences involving the actual practice of meditations. For those who wish to take up meditations, the basis for any genuine progress is to silence the tendency to treat the soul-spirit world as suitable for everyday conversation. While it may seem strange that Steiner wanted the student to take charge of his or her meditative exercises rather than the teacher, he put such an emphasis on human freedom in order to help the student realize whether or not he or she was truly ready for the path. He viewed a student's desire to have a teacher specify where and how to begin as evidence that the person was not yet ready for the path of initiation.

As with *Theosophy*, the study group for *Knowledge of Higher Worlds* had the good fortune of having a leader—actually two leaders—who plumbed its depths and wrote a book revealing their insights, complete with charts and diagrams. *How to Read a Book: A Study of "Knowledge of Higher Worlds"* by George and Gisela O'Neil takes the diagram of Unger for chapter one of *Theosophy* and shows it to be the organizing principle for the second basic book written in 1904. The O'Neils used Unger's method of composing topic sentences for each of the paragraphs in every chapter. They looked at the first chapter—"How is Knowledge of the Higher Worlds Attained?"—as a prelude made up of two groups of fourteen and nineteen paragraphs, with nodal points at paragraphs seven, fourteen, twenty-one, and twenty-seven. Chapter two, "The Stages of Initiation," relates to the physical body, through which we enter the sense world and meet the kingdoms of nature. Steiner explained in detail five sets of comparative meditations and described their effects, particularly the experience of the etheric bodies of plants and animals. He also warned of possible dangers. In a chart showing the ten exercises, the O'Neils summarized the corresponding steps forward both in spiritual perception and in moral development. Chapter three, "Initiation," is connected with the life

The First Period: 1902 - 1909

body. In their accompanying chart of the seven-year cycles in human biography, the O'Neils showed the three trials of initiation to be bound up with the sun period of human development from ages twenty-one to forty-two. Their pictures of the fire, water, and air trials are equally helpful in clarifying the importance of those three steps for advancing spiritual perception and attaining certain virtues.

In their exploration of chapter four, "Some Practical Aspects," the O'Neils compared their summaries of the twelve paragraphs to Ben Franklin's list of thirteen virtues. This helpful comparison sheds light on the relation of chapter four to the astral body and the idea of catharsis. An additional point of view might further clarify Steiner's intent in this chapter. The first two summary sentences seem introductory, and the last two seem to draw the chapter to a proper close. The middle eight summary sentences can be directly related to the eight virtues of the eightfold path. They are not in the same order as they later appear in chapter six, but some are clearly comparable—for example, "right word" with paragraph ten (be gentle in speech) and "right examination" with paragraph four (observe yourself and be honest). Just as chapter four relates to the eight-fold path, chapter five seems to be related to the sixfold path. In their chart of the summary sentences for the fifteen paragraphs of chapter five, the O'Neils identified the first three as preliminaries and the last five as summaries. The middle seven are connected with control of thinking, feeling, and willing (sentences four, six, and eight) and tolerance, open-mindedness, and inner balance (sentences five, nine, and ten). The last sentence—"the Real Self is found within"—embodies the ideal of freedom. Steiner's suggestions in *Guidance in Esoteric Training* for doing the exercises for the sixfold path advise the student to take up one exercise per month, but to refrain from doing any exercises in the seventh month. The O'Neils' summary for chapter five as a whole states: "Conditions for Soul Stability—Basis for <u>ALL</u> Progress on the Path." Rudolf Steiner stated the same idea in *Guidance in Esoteric Training* when discussing the sixfold path.[3]

Chapter six, "Some Results of Initiation," begins with a discussion of the effects of initiation that corresponds with the chapter's title. In the fourth paragraph, Steiner introduces the idea of chakras or lotus flowers and broaches the meaning of initiation as the lighting up and rotation of astral organs. Paragraph eight examines the throat chakra, or sixteen-

The First Period: 1902 - 1909

petal lotus flower, as a series of eight moral exercises or meditations. Steiner points out that his discussion of this series of exercises is the same as the one given by the Buddha for the eightfold path. The eleventh paragraph presents the sixfold path as the proper method of activating the heart chakra. Steiner also emphasizes that the six virtues must become the basis for a way of life. The fourteenth paragraph moves downward to the ten-petal and the six-petal lotus flowers—the solar plexus and the spleen chakras—and gives indications for how to develop the next higher stage of consciousness. In the age that will follow the present age of the consciousness soul, people will have a conscious experience of the human aura and attain the capacity for Imaginative consciousness.

The O'Neils suggested that the deeper meaning of chapter seven, "The Transformation of the Dream Life," involves the inner experience of the air trial by the consciousness soul. The human ego becomes active during its dreams at night and begins to bring order to them. The waking life is also transformed as the ego experiences the growth and unfolding of living thoughts ("building a hut") and attains decisiveness by receiving intimations of the guardian angel ("listening to the higher self"). The next chapter, "The

Continuity of Consciousness," is connected to the next higher member of man's essential being, the spirit self or higher self. Chapter eight thus relates to the practice of cultivating the ten-petal lotus flower and creating soul armor so that the human aura can appear in its glory at the stage of Imaginative consciousness. The ego then perceives the astral world not just by waking up in the dream life, but also by bringing dream experiences into everyday life.

The next chapter, "The Splitting of the Human Personality in Esoteric Training," points to the great psychological dangers faced by the student who would push on impatiently to ever-higher stages of knowledge. The ninth chapter describes the activation of the life spirit when the etheric or formative forces stream from the brow to the hands and form a network enclosing the etheric body. The accomplishment of this task, the actual birth of the higher self, is the reason that initiates in ancient times were called "the twice born" and that Christ Jesus said that one must be "born again in the spirit." The enclosure of the etheric body results in the gift of the "inner word." Steiner called this higher stage of knowledge "Inspiration," a conscious experience of the music of the spheres, which can be found in the compositions

THE FIRST PERIOD: 1902 - 1909

of master musicians, and the cosmic word, which resounds in the depths of the works of great writers. Chapter ten, "The Guardian of the Threshold," is likewise a warning. The admonition above the portal to the ancient temple at Delphi to "Know Thyself" requires true self-examination. Socrates insisted that the unexamined life is not worth living; nevertheless, the kind of honesty necessary to have the first true experience of Intuition, or communion with spiritual beings, is difficult to achieve. To know one's own faults and vices, to admit them and begin the slow process of reformation, is the prelude for the experience of the lesser guardian, sometimes called the double, or doppelgänger.

The O'Neils hinted at a deeper significance of *Knowledge of Higher Worlds* as a basic book. They indicated that chapter six, connected with the mind or intellectual soul, is packed with a plethora of details in a highly condensed form. The chapter seems to possess "the terse quality of a summary" because it indeed contains the whole path of anthroposophy within it. The O'Neils suggested that the asterisks following paragraph sixteen divide the chapter into two phases: the first phase covers the development of the astral organs of the soul, and the second phase relates to the

CHART IV

Knowledge of Higher Worlds—*Chapter 6*

Phase I: The lighting up and rotation of the chakras

¶ 1-3 — *Some Effects of Initiation (chap. 6)*
A student needs to know the effects of the meditative exercises.

¶ 4-7 — *Initiation (chap. 3)*
The exercises for the first three chakras assist the student with the fire, water, and air trials.

¶ 8-10 — *Practical Considerations (chap 4)*
The purification of the astral body through the eightfold path helps to activate the throat chakra.

¶ 11-13 — *Requirements for Esoteric Training (chap. 5)*
The protection of the sentient soul through the sixfold path activates the heart chakra. (The student's freedom is paramount except in the case of this exercise. The sixfold path must be carried out if any other meditation is to be undertaken.)

¶ 14-16 — *Achieving Continuity of Consciousness (chap. 8)*
The attainment of Imaginative consciousness through exercises to activate the solar plexus chakra gradually "transfers into waking consciousness the state we first formed out of our dream life."

Phase II: The etheric streams and the imprinting of astral organs

¶ 17-22 — *The Stages of Initiation (chap. 2)*
Exercises of concentration enabling the student to perceive the etheric body must begin by forming an etheric center in the head region so that the student can avoid becoming a dreamer. The center between the brows will move to the region of the larynx and bring illumination. Later the center will move near the physical heart.

¶ 23-24 — *The Splitting of the Personality in Esoteric Training (chap. 9)*
The movement of the etheric center to the region of the heart brings the gift of "the inner word." The appearance of the higher state of consciousness called Inspiration brings recognition of the depths of great writers like Buddha and St. John.

¶ 25-29 — *How to Know Higher Worlds (chap. 1)*
The four attributes develop an etheric center in the head region and assist its movement to, and maturity in, the heart region. These attributes are: distinguishing truth from appearance or opinion (reverence for truth); distinguishing the essential from the nonessential (an idea that becomes an ideal); the practice of the sixfold path (meditation as a daily exercise); and the love of freedom (discovery of the real self).

¶ 30-34 — *The Guardian of the Threshold (chap. 10)*
The experience of the lesser guardian requires the student to have undergone self-examination and to have learned to deal with oneself objectively.

¶ 35-38 — *Changes in the Dream Life of the Esoteric Student (chap. 7)*
The meeting with the higher self or spirit self requires the student to develop a feeling for the truth of the teachings of spiritual science. Listening to the higher self becomes the active use of the brow chakra in order to illumine the spiritual beings of the higher worlds.

¶ 39-43 — *The Greater Guardian of the Threshold (chap. 11)*
The gifts of developing the higher self include insight into the laws of reincarnation and karma and the existence of great initiates. Doubts about the spirit world cease, and religious services become images of our relationship to the spirit world.

imprinting of these upon the etheric or life body. The following chart attempts to illustrate the truth of the O'Neils' insights.

Steiner wrote a third basic book in 1904, which appeared in the members' magazine in the same fashion as had *Knowledge of Higher Worlds*. This collection of articles was finally published in book form in 1909 as *Cosmic Memory*. Its original title was *From the Akasha Chronicle*, and it told the story of the pre-historical events of the earth and of man. Rudolf Steiner was familiar with the findings of contemporary science and paleontology, having written articles on geology and the origin of the earth, and he was recognized as an expert in this field by a major encyclopedia. Having studied Western and Eastern spiritual traditions, he could also approach actual prehistoric events with spiritual vision, as *Knowledge of Higher Worlds* clearly suggests. His task was to mediate the extremes of modern materialistic science and the ancient Oriental texts. He accomplished this by introducing myths and other spiritual traditions into the sphere of prehistoric research. He has received no credit for building a foundation that led to a new era of prehistoric research.[4]

The First Period: 1902 - 1909

The task of bringing these two antithetical positions together in a basic book would not be fully reconciled until 1909 when Steiner published *Occult Science: An Outline*. *Cosmic Memory* (CW 11) represents a first step in this process. The original title shows the extent of the problem that Steiner faced. *From the Akasha Chronicle* makes use of obscure occult terminology. Steiner attempted to remedy this problem by comparing the memories of a human being to those of the universe—microcosmic memories to macrocosmic ones. He also referred to W. Scott-Elliott's *Story of Atlantis and Lemuria* to give the reader a frame of reference for the even more difficult task he faced in forming a new terminology for the great cycles and smaller sub-cycles that are at the heart of the occultist's view of prehistory. Steiner explained that the great cycles, called planets, referred to the development of different states of human consciousness, of which there will be seven states in all. Human beings attained trance consciousness, sleep consciousness, and dream consciousness in earlier stages of planetary evolution. Waking object consciousness is being developed in the present earth cycle, and Imagination, Inspiration, and Intuition will be attained in the future. Each planet is composed of seven sub-cycles, called rounds. Our present round is the mineral kingdom. Each round, or kingdom of life, is composed of seven globes, or conditions of form. Our present globe is the physical one, which will later ascend to an astral globe, and eventually to purely spiritual globes.

When Rudolf Steiner discussed Atlantis and Lemuria, he was referring to two of the seven root races that characterize the seven sub-cycles of a globe. Worse yet, the root races are themselves divided into seven sub-races. Steiner realized how such terminology could be used to foster and even propagate racism. As mentioned above, it was not until 1909 that Steiner was able to form a proper terminology suitable for the age of freedom. The research of modern natural science needed to be freed of its materialistic bias before it could be recast as spiritually imbued ideas to bring ancient doctrine and occult wisdom into the present day. In 1917, Steiner had to challenge those Western secret societies that insisted on misusing the terms Aryan root race and Anglo-Saxon sub-race to justify their racist ideology, which maintained that only white English-speaking people should play a leading role in the modern age. The difficulty that Steiner had with the language of root race and sub-race (which in *Occult Science* he will call epoch

The First Period: 1902 - 1909

and cultural age) should not diminish his insight into planets, rounds, and globes, and the hierarchies of spiritual beings that are active therein, nor his accomplishment in bringing such occult terminology into a spiritual form.

Peter Demay, the leader of the Friday night public study group of the Rudolf Steiner Group in Chicago, served as my mentor. He requested that I take on his role of group leader after his death. In 1983 I did so at the Grant Park location of the Rudolf Steiner Group. After leading the public study group for eleven years, I began teaching the basic books for Arcturus, the Waldorf teacher-training institute in Chicago. After ten more years I resumed leading a public study group for the Rudolf Steiner Branch, now located on Lincoln Avenue. I also taught the basic books for the Foundation Studies Program of Antioch College. Over the course of thirty-one years, I led discussions or taught courses on the basic books forty-two different times. Peter Demay believed that *Cosmic Memory* was a basic book. I have come to share his opinion that it is intended for the general public and does present a path to the higher worlds. Steiner even said that reading descriptions of the soul and spirit worlds is the best first step that can be taken on the path of knowledge. Imaginative consciousness can arise in a healthful way when one's soul enters into the inner conditions of prehistory. The pictures of earlier stages of evolution that Steiner was able to paint for his reader begin to act as a kind of roadmap and enable the student to begin to feel at ease with what truly is one's home.

Steiner wrote *Stages of Higher Knowledge* (CW 12) in 1906 as articles that were published in the German Section magazine. He intended these installments to be a continuation of *Knowledge of Higher Worlds*. In them, he identified the stages of knowledge that follow the three trials of initiation: Imagination, Inspiration, and Intuition. An important anthroposophist, Werner Glas, who became my mentor after Peter Demay's death, believed that *Stages* should have been included in *Knowledge of Higher Worlds*. I would agree that it was written for the general public and that it contains a further explanation of the path of knowledge building on the book that preceded it.

In chapter one of *Stages of Higher Knowledge*, Steiner discussed with philosophical exactness the stages of knowledge above the one of material cognition. The new terminology that he developed in his exploration of object, mental image, concept, and ego

The First Period: 1902 - 1909

has the clarity and logic of modern science. Not a vague or fanciful term, the word "Imagination" brings the actual goal and purpose of the next step in mankind's evolution into view. In chapter three Steiner examined why Imaginative knowledge needs to come first, before Inspirational knowledge. He made the danger of the ground slipping away beneath the student abundantly clear, and sounded a warning that the student must hear. In the second part of chapter six in *Knowledge of Higher Worlds*, Steiner had explained the decisive role that the sixfold path plays in attaining knowledge of higher worlds. He had emphasized the same idea in the title of chapter five of that book, "Requirements for Esoteric Training." In the second chapter of *Stages of Higher Knowledge*, Steiner showed that these six "subsidiary" exercises play an important role in bringing about a proper balance between the waking life and sleep. Only in the fourth and final chapter did Steiner introduce exercises appropriate for the development of Inspiration.

THE BASIC BOOKS OF RUDOLF STEINER

THE RELATION OF THE BASIC BOOKS TO THE MYSTERY STREAMS

Steiner was able to complete the task of uniting the path of Eastern esotericism with the transformed concepts of Western materialistic science in 1909. His "Autobiographical Sketch," also called the Barr document, was written in 1907. In it, Steiner told Edouard Schure about the reason he had taken on this task: "The occult powers standing behind me gave only the counsel: 'Everything in the clothing of Idealistic philosophy.'" When Steiner turned forty years of age in 1901, he could "appear publicly as a teacher of occultism, according to the intentions of the Masters." Until that time, he took on three specific problems in order to prepare for the public presentation of Rosicrucianism he would give at the beginning of the twentieth century. The signs of the times that he had to learn to read aright were Newton's theory of light based on spectral analysis; Darwin's theory of evolution of the organic world; and Mesmer's experiments with hypnotism and the discovery of trance consciousness.[5]

Steiner began his scientific studies at the University of Vienna at age eighteen. Three years later he

The First Period: 1902 - 1909

took employment as editor of Goethe's scientific writings for Kurschner's *German National Literature*. Working with Goethe's theory of color and his ideas of the archetypal plant and animal enabled Steiner to begin to solve the first two scientific problems. With Goethe's help, Steiner was able to develop "theosophical ideas in the gesture of a philosophic Idealism." In 1890, he continued his work on Goethe's scientific writings at the Goethe-Schiller Archives in Weimar, the city of Goethe.

With *Theosophy*, Steiner had clearly made progress in transforming Eastern nomenclature for the members of man's essential being to a Western spiritual scientific terminology. *Cosmic Memory* showed a similar advance in the naming of the classes of angels in the spiritual hierarchies and relating the greater cycles of cosmic evolution to a Western terminology. *Stages of Higher Knowledge* extended this success by naming the higher stages of initiation. Steiner's *Collected Works* reflect this steady progress and its culmination in *Occult Science: An Outline*. The basic books discussed up to this point are numbered successively from CW9 to CW12. The following chart indicates their relationship to *Occult Science: An Outline* (CW13).

CHART V

Relation of Occult Science *to the Basic Books of the Eastern Path*

CHAPTERS OF *OCCULT SCIENCE* (CW 13)	BASIC BOOKS OF THE EASTERN MYSTERY STREAM
1. The Character of Occult Science	*Theosophy* (CW9) Introduction
2. The Essential Nature of Mankind	*Theosophy* Chapter one — The Essential Nature of the Human Being
3. Sleep and Death	*Theosophy* Chapter two — Destiny and Reincarnation Chapter three — The Three Worlds
4. The Evolution of the Cosmos and Man	*Cosmic Memory* (CW11)
5. Cognition of the Higher Worlds — Initiation	*Knowledge of the Higher Worlds* (CW10) *Stages of Higher Knowledge* (CW12)
6. The Present and Future of Cosmic and Human Evolution	*Theosophy* Chapter three — The Human Aura

The First Period: 1902 - 1909

Hans Gebert, a colleague of Werner Glas at the Waldorf Teacher Training Institute in Southfield, Michigan, developed a chart to compare the terminology of the soul and spirit worlds in *Theosophy* with the spiritual scientific names used in chapter four of *Occult Science* (see chart III). Becoming familiar with the spiritual beings and the realms they inhabit can assist the student to understand their reappearances in later stages of evolution and how their new activity is at once a repetition and a higher stage of development. Hans believed that a serious student would want to create his or her own diagrams or charts of key events, — for example, the laying down of the seeds of the higher members of man's essential being in earlier planetary stages. The reason that Steiner called *Occult Science* "an outline" is that even a hundred pages of descriptions of cosmic evolution leaves an immense amount of work for the student. One of Steiner's foremost students in this regard was Gunther Wachsmuth, a member of the Executive Council at the time of the founding of the General Anthroposophical Society in 1924. Wachsmuth's research in his chosen field of natural science can be found in *Earth and Man, The Evolution of the Earth,* and *The Evolution of Mankind.*

THE BASIC BOOKS OF RUDOLF STEINER

Guenther Wachsmuth also took on a task prompted by the first sentence in the last chapter of Steiner's autobiography, *The Course of My Life*: "It will be difficult to separate what follows as an account of my life from the history of the Anthroposophical Movement."[6] This autobiographical account, which appeared in a series of weekly articles written for *The Goetheanum Newsletter*, related the events from Steiner's birth in 1861 up to the age of forty-six. Beginning in December of 1923, Steiner wrote seventy installments, the final one not published until five days after his death. Wachsmuth picked up where Steiner himself had left off, taking upon himself the enterprise of explaining the initiatives, lectures, and artistic projects that Steiner devoted himself to in the ensuing eighteen years. The organizing principle that Wachsmuth used was Steiner's own characterization of the seven-year periods involved in the growth and development of the Anthroposophical Movement. At the beginning of his biography, *The Life and Work of Rudolf Steiner,* Wachsmuth explained Steiner's viewpoint and presented certain details in an effort to characterize each of the three periods. The first period extended from 1902 to 1909, beginning with Steiner's entry into the Theosophical Society and ending with

The First Period: 1902 - 1909

his inner separation from it at the Budapest Congress. In this seven-year period Steiner wrote the first three basic books, which created an active spiritual life in the membership and led to the growth of the Anthroposophical Movement.

The Mystery Streams in Europe and the New Mysteries by Bernard Lievegoed helps to clarify the four major mystery streams.[7] This work provides an important framework for understanding how different paths of initiation evolved in each of the cultural ages in different parts of the earth and in the various peoples of the world. Lievegoed's last book, *The Battle for the Soul*, takes this effort a step further by showing how human beings in the present day, in keeping with the ideal of freedom, are taking on the leadership of these streams.[8] The first three basic books can be understood as a conscious effort on Steiner's part to bring the wisdom of the Eastern stream to the people of Europe and the West. Lievegoed provided the spiritual background for Steiner's endeavor by discussing Steiner's incarnation in the ninth century as Schionatulander, a Grail knight characterized in Wolfram von Eschenbach's *Parzival,* who had the mission of uniting the East and the West after the death of Gahmuret, Parzival's father. Bringing the wisdom of the Theosophical Society to the West required Steiner to make the Eastern path, the veneration of truth, accessible through the use of western concepts. His earlier incarnation was preparation for this task; *Theosophy, Knowledge of Higher Worlds*, and *Cosmic Memory* were the results.

Steiner also pursued the Goethe project in an attempt to transform the concepts of modern materialistic natural science into spiritual science. Lievegoed related this effort to Steiner's willingness to enter the Western stream, the mystery stream of willing, whose human leader is Christian Rosenkreutz. Steiner's incarnation as Thomas Aquinas enabled him to enter this stream and prepare the talents that he would need in order to make insights into spiritual realities accessible to human beings of the modern age through Western scientific concepts. With the publication of *Occult Science* in 1909, the defender of the faith in the late Middle Ages became the defender of natural science in the modern age.

Another event important to the Western stream of Rosicrucianism also occurred during the first period of the Anthroposophical Movement. In 1906, Steiner was invited to lead a Freemasonic Lodge. He accepted the certificate offered by John Yarker, but he

The First Period: 1902 - 1909

made it clear that he would establish his own symbolic ritual activity. Steiner had little interest in bolstering a "secret society" based on granting degrees and traditional ceremonies. Rather, he sought to present a visual picture of the path of the human soul ascending spiritually as part of a serious attempt to renew the sources of Freemasonry out of a modern, fully conscious, original investigation of spiritual reality. As early as 1904, Steiner gave lectures on the mysteries of Freemasonry in *The Temple Legend* (CW 93). He also discussed the architect of Solomon's Temple as an earlier incarnation of Rosenkreutz and expressed the hope that his efforts to renew Freemasonry might bear fruit in the future.

The first period of the Anthroposophical Movement focused on the development of active thinking through the study of the basic books of Rudolf Steiner. In his summary of printed works that appear during this period, Wachsmuth listed *Christianity as Mystical Fact* as the first book. It was given the number eight in the Collected Works of Rudolf Steiner. CW 9 to CW 12 were assigned to *Theosophy*, *Knowledge of Higher Worlds*, *Cosmic Memory*, and *Stages of Higher Knowledge*. CW 13 was given to *Occult Science*. Werner Glas wanted *Christianity as Mystical Fact* included in a pamphlet introducing new members of the Anthroposophical Society to the basic books. He viewed the presentation of the Christian path to the higher worlds as necessary orientation for an earnest seeker in the modern age.

Steiner began the lecture cycle that became *Christianity as Mystical Fact* in October 1901 at the Theosophical Society's library at the Brockdorff's home in Berlin. He felt little connection to the Theosophical Society's viewpoint because of the tendency of Oriental occultism to characterize Jesus as a minor prophet, in contrast to the great contributions of Siddhartha Gautama—who attained Buddhahood at the turn of the sixth century B.C.—and other spiritual leaders. After one of Steiner's lectures in November, Marie von Sivers asked him whether Theosophy did not need a Western-Christian spiritual movement to complement its Eastern emphasis. Steiner considered this question to be the outward justification for beginning just such a spiritual movement. When, at the end of the year, he was asked to join the Theosophical Society and take a leadership role in the German Section, he agreed to do so. His only condition was that Marie von Sivers work with him. *Christianity as Mystical Fact* was published in September 1902. The

The First Period: 1902 - 1909

German Section was founded the following month.

The full title of this basic book is *Christianity as Mystical Fact and the Mysteries of Antiquity*. The second chapter of the book examines the mystery centers where leaders like Heraclitus and Pythagoras prepared their pupils for initiation. What appeared in the myths of Heracles and Theseus, and in the epic of *The Odyssey*, as the journey to the underworld of Hades became the spiritual experience of these pupils at Ephesus and Samos. Such initiation was not for the many, but for the chosen few—the *mystae*, or the twice-born. The priests of the mystery centers placed restrictions upon the initiates; revealing the secrets of the mysteries was punishable by death, a fate that Aeschylus, the first great tragedian poet, almost suffered. The performances at the Theater of Dionysus were the high point of Greek culture. All Athenian citizens were required to attend the spring festival where the lesser mysteries—the soul ordeals of the fire trial, the water trial, and the air trial—were celebrated by playwrights like Aeschylus, Sophocles, and Euripides, who told the stories of the great Greek heroes.

In chapter three Steiner turned his attention to the form that the mysteries took in Plato's Academy. The figure of Socrates acting in accord with the higher self, the "daimon," allowed Plato to reveal the mystery of the air trial. What had appeared on stage as the drama of *Antigone* could now take the form of a dialogue. The sacred drama of Eleusis, however—the myth of Dionysos freeing Persephone from the chains of the Underworld—still had to remain hidden. In chapter five, Steiner turned to the Buddha. The greatness of the gifts of the Lord of Compassion—the eightfold path and the four noble truths—shone in the light of his union with the spirit, his transfiguration. Steiner discussed how Siddhartha Gautama's life fit the pattern of the great initiates. Such a correspondence provides the necessary proof for the stage of initiation that he attained.

Steiner next took up the transfiguration of Christ Jesus in chapter five and pursued the theme of Christ's development carefully throughout the following chapters. This event was not a conclusion of His earthly journey, but the start of a higher stage of development. Transfiguration Sunday leads to the mystery of Golgotha and the resurrection: "The life of Buddha demonstrated that the human being is in essence the divine Logos (Word); when our earthly part perishes, we return to the Logos, to the light. But in Jesus, the Logos takes on existence as an actual man, the Word

The First Period: 1902 - 1909

becomes flesh."[9] No longer does the human being have to search out a hidden mystery center to experience the outpouring of spirit in one's life. The spirit is open to all through the mystery of Golgotha, and the path of initiation can raise it to fully-awakened consciousness. The ancient mysteries prepared the human soul to rise up into the spiritual world to meet the spirit of the sun—the Idea of the Good, as Plato characterized Him in *The Republic*. The mystical fact of Christianity points to His appearance on the earth. The unfolding of the Spirit of Love in human souls is a gradual process. Steiner made clear that the ideal of the Kingdom of God—the blessed community that will arise—is not the exclusive right of a chosen few, but the shared experience of the spirit of brotherhood emerging within the human community.

The growth of the German Section of the Theosophical Society from 1902 to 1907 saw the membership increase to almost nine hundred. Steiner brought his spiritual research to the membership and to the public at large in response to real questions and concerns, in the same way that Marie von Sivers's question had opened a door for him to enter the Theosophical Society. The interest of members in the themes of *Christianity as Mystical Fact* led to his first lectures on the Gospels. He expanded his initial offerings over the following years into lecture cycles on *The Gospel of John* (CW 103), *The Gospel of Luke* (CW 114), *The Gospel of Matthew* (CW 123), and *The Gospel of Mark* (CW 139). Steiner believed that spiritual science could observe spiritual facts that stood behind these well-known writings, and could even help those who were estranged from religious life by the half-truths of natural science. Such pursuit of knowledge, however, had nothing to do with the wish to create a religion. Members of all religious faiths could be found in the membership rolls of the German Section, and spiritual science was only meant to serve in deepening such faith. Lecturing on the *Bhagavad-Gita*, for example, did not mean that Steiner wanted members to practice Hinduism.

THE PHILOSOPHY OF FREEDOM

The experience of conscience ushered in the modern age. The present age can be called the age of freedom because the inner voice takes precedence over external authorities. The thunderclap of conscience first sounded through Luther and the beginning of the Protestant Reformation. John Calvin

The First Period: 1902 - 1909

and John Knox further developed Luther's ideas in the fields of theology, public education, and church organization. In the first half of the eighteenth century, John Wesley extended Protestantism's influence through structured study groups and measured self-development. The method he used gave rise to the name of the denomination associated with him—Methodism. By 1750, another shift began to occur, and advances in the religious sphere gave way to new creations in the artistic realm and the cultural sphere. The essays of Herder and Lessing led to the plays of Schiller and the poetry and novels of Goethe. By the 1790s the philosophic works of Fichte, Schelling, and Hegel appeared and lent the name of Idealism to the cultural movement in Germany.

Just as Protestantism spread from Germany into the Low Countries, then northward into Scandinavia and England, so too Idealism. Wordsworth and Coleridge introduced Idealism to England with their book of poems, *Lyrical Ballads*. They named it Romanticism, and it influenced novelists, essayists, and especially poets. Channeling this inspiration, Keats, Shelley, and Byron brought English poetry to new heights. This cultural movement even crossed the Atlantic Ocean and ushered in the beginning of

The Basic Books of Rudolf Steiner

American culture, where it was called Transcendentalism. Emerson and Thoreau played the roles that Goethe and Schiller had for Germany, and that Wordsworth and Coleridge had for England. In his essay "Transcendentalism" Emerson explained that, to the question of "What is Transcendentalism," the answer was simply "Idealism in Boston in the 1840s."

The waning of Transcendentalism in 1850 signaled the completion of the mission to found a culture that could prepare free human beings to carry out their future tasks. The foundations laid by Protestantism and Idealism at the beginning of the modern age can be compared to the foundations of the classical age laid down by the epics of Homer and the masterworks of the tragedians and philosophers of Ancient Greece. The Barr document was discussed earlier with regard to Steiner's research on Goethean science. Also called "An Autobiographical Sketch," it emphasized Steiner's devotion to Idealism and maintained that Steiner's own spiritual mentor insisted on establishing complete accord with the height of modern culture: "Everything in the clothing of Idealistic philosophy." Only in that manner could freedom be safeguarded for readers of Steiner's early works. Among the rules of conduct that Steiner had to

The First Period: 1902 - 1909

observe was the demand that he not reveal any occult knowledge publicly until he reached the age of forty. He had to follow this rule until 1901, just as he had to refuse to put his own ideas or plans into action until a request to do so had come from another person. The question of Marie von Sivers about whether a Christian element could be brought together with the Theosophical movement can thus be seen in its proper light. In simplest terms, Steiner's own conduct exemplifies the principle that occult powers and faculties must never be used for personal reasons. They are meant to serve all of mankind.

The *Collected Works* that appeared in printed form before 1900 were numbered CW 1 to CW 6. They basically focused on Goethe's worldview, his study of nature, and Nietzsche's freedom philosophy. The one exception was Steiner's own philosophic work, *The Philosophy of Freedom* (CW 4), which was published in 1894. Steiner attempted to address the fundamental questions of the modern age: What is freedom and how can we act freely? He did so in the tradition of Hegel's *Philosophy of History*, which tried to show history as the unfolding of the idea of freedom, and of Schelling's *Of Human Freedom*, which examined freedom as exercised by the individual human being. Steiner took these two greatest works of Idealism and built upon them. When he formed a publishing company in 1905—the Philosophical-Anthroposophical Publishing Company—the second book he published was *The Philosophy of Freedom*. Despite the difficulties involved, Steiner bought the remaining copies and the publishing rights from his old publisher. Much later he explained that, of all the forty-five books and six thousand lectures that he had given, only *The Philosophy of Freedom* would stand the test of time. He envisioned that it would provide future generations a millennium from now the insight and inspiration they would need in order to master the soul trial of our age and attain to the sphere of freedom

In *The Philosophy of Freedom*, Rudolf Steiner blazed a path of thinking that did not require admonishments about the danger of blind faith, or warnings about the hazards of occult exercises done without full knowledge of the proper manner of carrying them out, or cautions about doing them in ignorance of their possible physical and psychic effects. The proper passageway to living thoughts and communion with spiritual beings lies through active thinking that forms intuitions and creates a first-hand experience of the

The First Period: 1902 - 1909

truthfulness of Steiner's words, not employing intellectual, academic thinking. Peter Demay told me that *The Philosophy of Freedom* had enabled him to attain spirit vision. It is in that sense—as a bridge from the earthly realm to the spiritual world and as a book written for the general public—that *The Philosophy of Freedom* is a basic book. Although it was written before the first period of the Anthroposophical Movement—when *Christianity as Mystical Fact, Theosophy, Knowledge of Higher Worlds*, and *Occult Science—An Outline* were written and published—*The Philosophy of Freedom* remains to this day the largest selling basic book in Germany.

The Philosophy of Freedom is divided into two parts. The first part is a discussion of the knowledge of freedom. Peter Demay explained to me that Steiner's path of knowledge is a reversal of the Eastern path of yoga, which begins with the activation of the kundalini fire in the region of the root chakra and proceeds upward until the crown chakra becomes active. The Western path of knowledge begins by directing the soul force of thinking to the question of conscious human action. The crown chakra becomes active when the individual begins to realize that action becomes conscious when thinking provides a motive.

The second chapter leads the student by logic to the conclusion that the desire for knowledge is fundamental because the world of nature and the spiritual world appear as a duality. Following this activation of the brow chakra, connected with Jupiter, comes chapter three. The development of the throat chakra is bound up with the influence of Mars and the world-soul-mood of voluntarism. The pupil on the path of knowledge now discovers that thinking serves knowledge when it is a purely willed activity and directly experienced as such. It is this experience that Descartes was pointing to when he ushered in the modern age of philosophy with "cogito ergo sum." Not all people of the present day can wake up, as it were, in their own thinking activity. Yet without such active, living thoughts, the rest of Part I must fall on deaf ears.

Chapter four takes up the question of the perception of the world and considers the problem that Immanuel Kant caused for all of modern philosophy. Steiner cuts through the Kantian knot, so that rays of light can begin to shine from the astral organ in the region of the heart. The mystical union that occurs when percept and concept join together in the act of knowing—explored in chapter five—brings activity

The First Period: 1902 – 1909

to the next chakra, the one in the region of the solar plexus that is related to the Venus mysteries. In chapter six, the human individuality connects percepts coming from the outer world to the subject and discovers that the ego also gives life to concepts. The power of memory and the activity of thinking transcend nature and the spirit, which together enliven the spleen chakra. The final chapter of part one shows that monism recognizes only time, space, and defects in the human organism as limits to knowledge. The following chart of the first seven chapters is based on a conversation with Peter Demay.

Peter suggested that, having followed the idea of freedom down into the depths, the student would retrace a mirror path by moving gradually upward, experiencing the reality of freedom in the process. Chapter eight, like chapter seven, falls under the world-soul-mood of occultism. It presents the experience of intuition penetrating the world's phenomena. The Factors of Life, as the chapter is titled, include living, active thinking—the pure thinking of the philosophers. The next chapter moves into the worldview of Transcendentalism and shows that a pure action can derive from just such a pure thought. Such a motive transcends the phenomenal world and

CHART VI

The Philosophy of Freedom
Part I: The Knowledge of Freedom

Chapters	World-Soul Moods	Astral organs and Atlantean oracles
1. Conscious Human Action	Gnosticism	Crown chakra (Saturn Oracle)
2. The Fundamental Desire for Knowledge	Logicism	Brow chakra (Jupiter Oracle)
3. Thinking in the Service of Knowledge	Voluntarism	Throat chakra (Mars Oracle)
4. The World as Percept	Empiricism	Heart chakra (sun oracle)
5. The Act of Knowing	Mysticism	Solar plexus chakra (Venus mysteries)
6. Human Individuality	Transcendentalism	Spleen chakra (Mercury mysteries)
7. Are There Limits to Knowledge	Occultism	Root chakra (Vulcan mysteries)

The First Period: 1902 - 1909

points to the spiritual origin of a free deed, which finds its source in the moral world order. Freedom-philosophy reveals the truth of monism. Chapter ten allows the student on this path of knowledge to experience mysticism, the corresponding unity of concept and percept attained when a moral thought is brought into the world and made manifest as a free deed.

Peter invited a leading anthroposophist from England to come speak to the Rudolf Steiner Group in Chicago. Michael Wilson, who translated *The Philosophy of Freedom* into English, came in 1981 and presented an alternate but complementary viewpoint towards Part II. Michael tended to use the terminology developed by Carl Unger in *Language of the Consciousness Soul* to discuss the stages of a free deed. Rather than emphasizing the world-soul-moods, Michael focused on the spiritual faculties being developed in each chapter. From this point of view, chapter ten portrays the creation of a moral thought by means of the faculty of pure thinking—a moral intuition. Chapter eleven clarifies how difficult it can be to bring a moral intuition into the world—that it can that months, years, and even decades. The faculty required to persevere and to hold onto a moral intuition can be called Love for the Objective. The title of chapter twelve names the faculty needed to bring a Moral Intuition down into the soul realm. Moral Imagination converts a pure thought into a picture, or image, so that it can enter the souls of other men and women to inspire them as well. Fully realizing this ideal requires that it be brought down to the most practical level—the plane of everyday life where common sense prevails and where tasks are accomplished. Michael called this activity of the intellectual or mind soul Moral Technique. The following chart characterizes the stages of a free deed in accord with his lecture.

In his autobiography Steiner stated: "In the Theosophical Society, *there was no lingering doubt* that I would present only the results of my own direct, spiritual investigations."[10] At the inaugural meeting of the German Section, he had to leave early in order to give a lecture to a non-theosophical audience. He added these words to the title: "An Anthroposophy." The following day, Annie Besant, the leader of the Theosophical Society, granted Rudolf Steiner and Marie von Sivers membership in the Esoteric School. Steiner soon established correspondence with other members in Germany. In 1904 he was named "Arch Warden of the Esoteric School" for Germany, with the

CHART VII

The Philosophy of Freedom
Part II: The Reality of Freedom

Chapters	Unger's terms in *Language of the Consciousness Soul*	Wilson's terms for the Stages of a Free Deed
8. The Factors of Life	willing of Thinking	pure thinking (or causality)
9. The Idea of Freedom	willing of Feeling	substance of the moral world order
10. Freedom-philosophy And Monism	willing of Willing	Moral Intuition
11. World Purpose and Life Purpose	feeling of Willing	Love of the Objective
12. Moral Imagination	thinking of Willing	Moral Imagination
13. The Value of Life	mind soul (realizes a moral deed)	Moral Technique
14. Individuality and Genius	spiritual soul (knows the motive of an action)	ideal of spiritual research

right to admit new members. Steiner acted out of freedom in administering the Esoteric School through lectures and rituals, just as he would work out his own symbolic ritual activity two years later when he took on the task of renewing Freemasonry (see CW 264-266).

The demand for autonomy, to be able to act in freedom, was prerequisite to Steiner's attempt to renew esoteric traditions and make them amenable to mankind in the present age. For those students of Steiner who believe that reading a basic book of his and carrying out its suggestions will lead somewhere positive, a serious study of *The Philosophy of Freedom* may be recommended. Steiner expected his students to decide for themselves what needed to be done, as well as when and how. Lievegoed viewed Steiner as the great initiate who became the leader of the path of thinking, just as Parzival had done for the path of feeling and Rosenkreutz for the path of willing. Lievegoed stressed that even these highest initiates needed to unite with mystery streams other than their own to achieve the requisite harmony of feelings and inner balance of soul. Steiner's own incarnations in the Eastern and Western mystery streams in medieval Europe were discussed earlier. Lievegoed pointed to Steiner's more ancient incarnation as Aristotle—

The First Period: 1902 - 1909

whom Dante called "the master of those who know"—as the basis for his leadership of the Northern mystery stream of thinking. The founder of philosophy itself returned to modern Europe to bring the stream of philosophy to a proper conclusion and usher it in anew as anthroposophy.

The following chart summarizes Steiner's activity as the founder of the Anthroposophical Movement and the author of the basic books, organized according to the three mystery streams that Lievegoed discussed in *The Battle for the Soul*, as well as a fourth stream connected to an incarnation of Steiner in Ancient Greece before the time of Aristotle. Lievegoed could have related the pre-Socratic philosopher, Cratylus, to the mysteries of antiquity, and especially to the temple of Diana at Ephesus.

CHART VIII

The Basic Books and the First Period of the Anthroposophical Movement (1902 — 1909)

STEINER

| NORTHERN STREAM |

ARISTOTLE

The Philosophy of Freedom
(CW 4) — 1894

Founding the German Section
of the Theosophical Society
1902

Founding the First Section of
the Esoteric School
(CW 264-266) — 1904

ROSENKREUTZ

| WESTERN STREAM |

AQUINAS

Founding a
Freemasonic Lodge
1906

Occult Science
(CW13) — 1909

PARZIVAL

| EASTERN STREAM |

SCHIONATULANDER

Theosophy
(CW 9) — 1904

Knowledge of Higher Worlds
(CW 10) — 1904

Stages of Higher Knowledge
(CW 12) — 1906

Cosmic Memory
(CW 11) — 1904

MASTER JESUS

| SOUTHERN STREAM |

CRATYLUS

Christianity as Mystical Fact
(CW 8) — 1902

Lectures on the Bible
(CW 103-4, 114)
1907 — 1909

PART II:
THE RENEWAL OF THE ARTS AND THE SECOND PERIOD OF THE ANTHROPOSOPHICAL MOVEMENT

1909-1916

THE NORTHERN MYSTERY STREAM AND THE ACTIVITY OF ANTHROPOSOPHIA

Guenther Wachsmuth said that the second period of the Anthroposophical Movement began with the publication of *Occult Science: An Outline*. I instead included this work in the first period, which emphasized the soul force of thinking and the study of the basic books. The second period relates to the soul force of feeling and is usually called the period of the renewal of the arts. Wachsmuth called it "the realization of the unity of science, art, and religion." He identified the four key activities of this seven-year cycle as the writing of the Mystery Dramas, the birth of Eurythmy, the dramatic presentations from Goethe's *Faust*, and the construction of the first Goetheanum.

Four important written works were published from the years 1911 to 1913. The first three were

THE BASIC BOOKS OF RUDOLF STEINER

included in the *Collected Works* of Rudolf Steiner with the numbers CW 15, CW 16, and CW 17. The fourth work was published in 1912, but was added as CW 40 when the *Collected Works* were assembled. The first one, *The Spiritual Guidance of the Individual and Humanity* (CW 15), reproduces the content of the lectures that Steiner gave in 1911 in Copenhagen. In the preface, he wrote that the lectures presupposed familiarity with *Theosophy* and *Occult Science*.[1] Thus, *Spiritual Guidance* is not a basic book. It was not intended for the general public, nor does it present a complete path to the higher worlds. It is similar to *Christianity as Mystical Fact* in that it was first delivered as lectures and was then revised. Its style, however, was not changed, and it remains closer to Steiner's spoken word. Its content also resembles that of *Christianity as Mystical Fact* in that Steiner explored the role of the Christ as the spirit guide of the child from the time of birth to age three. Steiner also discussed His activity in artistic creations, the healing forces, and the powers of higher knowledge, as well as His reappearance in the etheric world. Steiner also elucidated the mystery of the two Jesus children, the miraculous change that occurred in the temple at the age of twelve, and the appearance of the

The Second Period: 1909 - 1916

dove during His baptism by John at age thirty. All these insights serve as a backdrop for His role as Spirit Guide in the present age, the fifth cultural age of the consciousness soul and mankind's attainment of freedom. Though not a basic book, *The Spiritual Guidance of the Individual and Humanity* is more like an advanced course for students who have taken up the path of the Southern mystery stream.

A Way of Self-Knowledge (CW 16) was written in 1912 and contains eight meditations. It too lacks the qualities of a basic book. In his "Introductory Remarks" to the book, Rudolf Steiner said, "*A Way of Self-Knowledge* supplements and amplifies my earlier work *How to Know Higher Worlds*."[2] For those who have set foot upon the Eastern path of initiation, these meditations—each one about nine pages in length—can be viewed as an advanced course. *The Threshold of the Spiritual World* (CW 17), written the following year, contains sixteen aphorisms, each an average of six pages in length. Steiner's "Introductory Remarks" tell the reader that *The Threshold* is not a basic book—that it "is intended to be neither systematic nor complete."[3] He compares it to *A Way of Self-Knowledge* and says it "should be considered supplementary to my other works." Its aphoristic form suggests that it is related to the Northern path of philosophy/anthroposophy, while its content includes descriptions of the soul's experiences in the elemental and spiritual worlds related to those presented in *Theosophy* and *Occult Science*. The sixteenth aphorism explains Steiner's view of this relationship and indicates how *The Threshold of the Spiritual World* serves as a kind of advanced course.

Steiner published *The Calendar of the Soul* in 1912, but it is included in *Truth-Wrought-Words* (CW 40) in the *Collected Works*. The fifty-two verses for meditation on the weeks of the year are as different from the prose of the basic books as the lectures, meditations, and aphorisms of the three books just discussed—perhaps even more so. These verses may be accurately compared to the mantrams that Steiner presented to his students in the Esoteric School and in the Freemasonic Lodge. The Soul Calendar verses are composed in such a way that each sound has a deep significance. Just as a great poet would insist that every word has to be in precisely the right place—like a jewel in its setting, — for the poem to succeed, an author of a mantram would speak in a similar way of each and every syllable. *The Calendar of the Soul* does lay out a complete path to the higher worlds, but not

The Second Period: 1909 - 1916

a path that the general public could be expected to understand. Neither are the dangers of this path clearly addressed. To approach the secrets of the Northern mystery stream in freedom and with insight would require a transformation of thinking like that provided by the study of *The Philosophy of Freedom*.

Fortunately, one of Rudolf Steiner's pupils, Karl Konig, wrote *Rudolf Steiner's The Calendar of the Soul — A Commentary*. His book serves as a kind of intermediary between the depths of the mystery wisdom of the earth and its revelation in the cycle of the year. Konig helps the student who wishes to plumb such depths with something more than reverent devotion by providing enlightened thoughts and insights. In chapter two, Konig unveils the secret of the birth in the human soul of the faculty of boding, or foreseeing future events. Equally wondrous spiritual truths of the present age appear in the other five chapters. For those students inclined to further research, Konig's book provides a method for unearthing many more such secrets.

Rudolf Steiner's *The Calendar of the Soul* is bound up with the founding of the Anthroposophical Society, which took place in 1912. When he founded the German Section of the Theosophical Society in

1902, Steiner had hoped that it could eventually become the Anthroposophical Section. In 1909, at the conclusion of the first period of the movement's development, Steiner again gave lectures on anthroposophy that framed the annual general meeting in a manner similar to what he had done at its founding seven years earlier. The difference, as Wachsmuth observed, was that a decisive inner separation had occurred at the Budapest conference.[4] Although the end was clearly coming, the formal separation from the Theosophical Society did not take place until the annual general meeting of 1911. Steiner wanted the members to decide for themselves whether they would join with him in opposing the Star of the East and its declaration that a young boy, Krishnamurti, was the reincarnation of Christ—a belief decreed as a condition for remaining a member of good standing in the Theosophical Society. The membership of the German Section agreed to leave the Theosophical Society and form a new one. The following year, in the first week of September, the Anthroposophical Society was founded. A week later, with Steiner's visit to Dornach, Switzerland, the preparations for the entrance of Anthroposophia onto the stage of world history were complete.

The Second Period: 1909 - 1916

A proper understanding of the spiritual being of Anthroposophia can be gleaned from the next book that Steiner published. *The Riddles of Philosophy* (CW 18) appeared in 1914. It is a basic book, since it fits the criteria of being written for the general public, requiring no specialized terminology, and containing a complete path for the attainment of knowledge of the higher worlds. As a further development of *The Philosophy of Freedom*, Steiner had written *Conceptions of the World and of Life in the Nineteenth Century*, a two-volume work that was his last before he began to write his anthroposophical works. *Conceptions of the World* had deepened his exploration of Idealism and had included a survey of the fields of philosophy and literature in the nineteenth century. In his autobiography, Steiner insisted that he did not progress through a series of contradictory positions, but rather that he advanced from one stage to the next by discovering new realms—that his spiritual development was, in other words, entirely consistent.[6] With the founding of the German Section in 1902, *The Philosophy of Freedom* became the basic book of the Northern mystery stream, as shown in chart VIII. With the advance to the second period of the movement's development, a basic book needed to arise that was in tune not just with philosophic Idealism, but also with anthroposophy itself. Steiner expanded his earlier two-volume work on the philosophy of the nineteenth century to include the history of philosophy, beginning with its origin in the pre-Socratic philosophers of Ancient Greece. *The Riddles of Philosophy* might seem like an advanced course rather than a basic book; indeed, for students without a connection to the path of thinking, the thought of reading the history of philosophy might seem daunting. Yet consider what a student of philosophy might think when he or she is told to take up the path of feeling and practice the meditations given in *Knowledge of Higher Worlds*. How might a person rooted in thinking react to being told that their feeling life must change in fundamental ways if they seek entrance to the path of veneration—that meditations themselves are fruitless without first fostering a proper soul mood? The different paths of initiation exist because human beings are so various, and in the present age people really do tend to a certain one-sidedness in their soul life. The truth of initiation is that it can only be properly achieved by overcoming the tendency towards a one-sided development of a particular force soul at the expense of the other two. The reason

The Second Period: 1909 - 1916

Steiner had to write so many basic books attests to the extent of the problem. He did not expect to solve it. From his viewpoint, a real solution would require several incarnations. He did hope to prepare the way for a solution by fostering a positive attitude within the student to work on one's own weaknesses and seek for harmony by balancing the three soul forces.

Fortunately, the study of *The Riddles of Philosophy* need not be hopelessly long or exceedingly boring. A leading anthroposophist, Rudolf Grosse, took up the task that Carl Unger and George and Gisela O'Neil accomplished for *Theosophy* and *Knowledge of Higher Worlds*. He unveiled the organizing principle of *Riddles of Philosophy* and allowed a deep insight to light up within the student of this basic book. His book, *The Living Being "Anthroposophia,"* culminates with a chart of the seven-hundred-year cycles of Philosophia's development, the archangelic counterpart of the seven-year cycles of human development.[7] The final chapter of Steiner's basic book is entitled "A Brief Outline of an Approach to Anthroposophy." Steiner stated outwardly what Rudolf Grosse carefully assisted the reader to experience inwardly—that the metamorphosis of Philosophia into Anthroposophia is the great secret of the present age.

The Basic Books of Rudolf Steiner

THE HERALDS OF THE MICHAEL AGE IN WORLD LITERATURE

In order to grasp this transformation concretely, the student should consult another book of Steiner's. It is the only book other than *The Spiritual Guidance of the Individual and Mankind* (CW 15) that Steiner presented first in the form of lectures and later revised.[8] *The Mission of Individual Folk Souls* (CW 121) first appeared as lectures delivered from June 7-17, 1910, which Steiner later amended. In this lecture cycle, he focused on two significant spiritual beings and their activity in Ancient Greece. The first was Apollo, the time-spirit or archai, who founded the Greco-Roman cultural age. Certain angelic beings, namely Calliope and Melpomene, assisted him by inspiring Homer ("O Muse, speak through me the wrath of Achilles") and the tragic poets discussed above. The time of Apollo's rulership lasted from around 750 B.C. to 400 B.C. The modern age, which Steiner also called the Central European age, may be compared to Apollo's rulership, since it also lasted about 350 years, beginning around 1500 and culminating on the shores of the new world with the end of Transcendentalism around 1850.

THE SECOND PERIOD: 1909 - 1916

The second spiritual being that Steiner discussed extensively in *The Mission of Individual Folk Souls* was Michael, a spirit of the age. Michael can also be called a planetary archangel. He has ruled as the leader of the sun oracle since the time of ancient Atlantis, and he also played a significant role as the Lord of Hosts during the time of the Exodus from Egypt. Along with the sun regent, the archangels of Saturn, Venus, Jupiter, Mercury, Mars, and the moon alternate as they ascend to the office of spirit of the age, each ruling for a span of 365 years. Michael last ruled around the same time that Apollo rose to prominence in Ancient Greece. It was he who stood behind the activity of Philosophia—evident in the activity of the pre-Socratic thinkers, the Academy of Plato, and the Lyceum of Aristotle—in the same manner that Apollo did the Muses. Thus these two beings worked in harmony to foster the birth of Western culture. The sun regency of Michael in Ancient Greece began in 676 B.C. and ended in 311 B.C. The glory that was Greece points to this convergence of the two spiritual beings. Steiner also discussed how these two leaders of the third hierarchy of angels took on the task of preparing one of the Germanic folk souls of that ancient time to usher in a future culture that would assist in realizing freedom in the following age. Steiner would call this future archai the Central European time spirit—Idealism.

A significant difference between the time of Greek classical culture and that of modern Idealism is that the sun regency was not active during the latter. Steiner explained that although the time of the sun regency in the modern age had not yet arrived, Michael could yet be active in the mystery streams of Grail Christianity and Rosicrucianism, especially in their cultural manifestations in *Parzival* and the plays of Shakespeare. Philosophia also continued her activity down through the ages, which reached a certain height in the philosophers of German Idealism. Yet the new Michael age had to wait until the end of Idealism's aegis in 1850, so that six times three hundred and sixty-five years would pass after the end of the previous Michael age in 311 B.C. Only in 1879 would the sun regency's beneficent and radiant influence begin to shine again, this time over the age of the consciousness soul.

The appearance of certain literary works at the beginning of the 1880s heralded the dawn of the new Michael age. Steiner described how a spirit of the age "gives his commissions to the Folk-spirits, so that the collective spirit of the age is specialized, individualized

The Second Period: 1909 - 1916

by the Folk-spirits."[9] Dostoyevsky began this process in 1879 by writing his masterpiece, *The Brothers Karamazov*, which was published in 1880. Thus did the folk soul of Russia help found the new age. The following year Ibsen began writing the work that culminated the second period of his creative activity. *An Enemy of the People*, by Norway's great dramatist, can be viewed as the Norwegian folk soul's further development of the ideal of freedom. In 1879, Samuel Clemens, giving voice to the American folk soul, began writing his masterpiece, *The Adventures of Huckleberry Finn*. It was finally completed in 1884. In 1882, Nietzsche began writing *Thus Spake Zarathustra*. His masterpiece, like Mark Twain's, was published in 1884. The geographical locations of those folk souls who answered the call of freedom suggest Europe's pivotal role in the present cultural age. Russia and America represent the eastern and western elements and form the horizontal axis, while Norway and Germany can be viewed as the northern and southern elements forming the vertical axis of a cross.

The nature and content of the call to freedom can be discovered in these works of world literature. The heroes of these works embody the new element about to enter civilization itself. These heroes are representatives of the emerging consciousness soul, the full development of which is the mission of the Central European cultural age. As fully developed, rounded characters, they can enter into the souls of men and women and assist those human beings who would respond to the call to freedom. Zarathustra seeks for the basis of his action within himself. He exemplifies the stage of a free deed called Moral Intuition (see chart VII). Alyosha, in *The Brothers Karamazov*, shows the fervor of spiritual striving in his devotion to his teacher and then to his brothers. He is representative of the stage called Love for the Objective. Dr. Stockman, in *An Enemy of the People*, possesses a multitude of new ideas to help transform society, an abundance of concrete initiatives that Zarathustra and Alyosha seem to lack. His character expresses the creativity of the Moral Imagination. Stockman, however, is unable to realize these ideas in a practical way. The stage of Moral Technique, so lacking in him, is to be found in Huck Finn. Demonstrating practicality in every conceivable way, Huck still has to struggle to attain the most basic of moral ideas. Thus do the folk souls specialize and individualize the Michaelic call to freedom. Through the heroes of these four masterworks at the dawn of the new Michael age,

The Second Period: 1909 - 1916

the folk-spirits point mankind to the reality of freedom manifest in the four stages of a free deed.

These heroes also present pictures of the danger of one-sided soul development. Like Thomas Stockman working with Petra, or Alyosha with his brothers, free human beings must avoid the pitfall of going it alone. The danger of becoming an enemy of the people can only be gradually overcome by recognizing one's own weaknesses and the need for friends and colleagues. The call to freedom includes the demand to take up the path of initiation. The trials of these heroes show how protection is granted to those who are on the path, and how strength is given to those who are tested. This message to mankind through the folk souls of the peoples also sounds a note of warning. This clarion call resounds especially through Dostoyevsky. The legend of the Grand Inquisitor tells of the false Messiah tempting mankind. This revelation of Satan's nature is the culmination of Dostoyevsky's life.[10] He died but three months after completing *The Brothers Karamazov* while working on its sequel, a book that was to encompass the events in Alyosha's life after the age of thirty-five. The fates of Friedrich Nietzsche and Samuel Clemens should also serve as a warning of what Steiner called the occult background of this age of freedom—that the fall of the spirits of darkness did in fact accompany Michael's defeat of the dragon. The lives of these two authors show how deadly real is this battle between Christ and the adversary forces in the hearts of men.

Full clarity about the founding of the sun regency in 1879 requires understanding the transformations of both Philosophia and Michael. *The Mission of Individual Folk Souls* (CW 121) explains the change in Michael. He leaves the archangelic class of the spiritual hierarchies and ascends to the next higher class—that of the archai, or the time spirits, who Steiner also calls the Spirits of Personality. Though no longer a planetary archangel and the regent of the sun, Michael now serves the same spiritual beings that he always had, but without being limited to a certain people (as he served for the tribes of Israel in the Egyptian cultural age or the Celtic peoples in the Greco-Roman age) or for a certain span of time (as with the Michael age). *The Riddles of Philosophy* took on the task of explaining which angelic being was specially prepared to take Michael's place and ascend to the office of the planetary archangel of the sun. Philosophia left the rank of the angels and no longer inspires individual

The Second Period: 1909 - 1916

human beings, but is now a planetary archangel working in the unconscious soul realms of every human being to inspire a love of freedom. Her presence is the reason that even those people who would serve the Grand Inquisitor must feign their love of freedom in their efforts to enslave mankind.

The new Michael age is actually the sun regency of Philosophia. Steiner tried to explain that it is also something else. *The Calendar of the Soul* pointed to this mystery in the motto that it bore: "1879 after the birth of the I am." For Steiner, this motto meant that the publication of *The Soul Calendar* was actually 1879 years after the Mystery of Golgotha in 33 A.D., the turning point in time when the Christ "I am" united itself with the spirit of the earth to undertake its renewal and redemption.[11] The seed that was born in 1 A.D. at Christmastide bore fruit thirty-three years later. This pattern is woven into the fabric of time such that the genesis of an idea can mature and manifest as a deed after that period of time. Historians might at some point study such occurrences and make note of the fact that Benjamin Franklin published the Albany Plan in 1754 and participated in the Constitutional Convention in 1787; or that Mohandas Gandhi returned to India in 1915 to lead the independence movement, which resulted in India's freedom in 1948. For Steiner, the secret of the year 1879 was bound up with the dawn of the new Michael age. It bore fruit thirty-three years later in 1912 with the founding of the Anthroposophical Society. Steiner attempted to make plain that what Aristotle had once founded in the classical age as philosophy could now to be taken up in freedom as anthroposophy, united with the soul, and put into practice in order to become the basis for the free deeds of modern men and women.

The coming of Steiner's fortieth year meant that he could appear before the world as an initiate, as was mentioned earlier in connection with the founding of the German Section in 1902. It also coincided with an event similar to that of the dawn of the new sun regency, after an interval of over two thousand years. This second event, however, was five millennia in preparation. The Ancient Greek term for it is the end of the Iron Age, while the Hindus refer to it as the end of the Kali Yuga—the end of the Age of Darkness and the birth of the Age of Light. After the year 1899, spiritual light began to shine on the earthly realm as the doors of heaven slowly began to swing open again. For occultists, this momentous occurrence signified that esoteric wisdom, so long withheld

The Second Period: 1909 - 1916

from the majority of mankind, could now be revealed. Specifically, the trials of initiation could now be spoken of publicly, the higher stages of initiation could be indicated, and exercises for their attainment could be given.

The chart that follows may be helpful in providing a picture of the activity of Apollo and Michael in the founding of Greek culture as well as the activity of Idealism and Michael in founding the culture of Central Europe. A more complete explanation of this latter activity would require a study of Michael's role as the spirit of esoteric Christianity and how he fostered both the Eastern Grail stream and the Western Rosicrucian stream. A description of this archangelic activity of Michael can be found in *The Missions of Individual Folk Souls* and related lectures. The third column in this chart attempts to relate the founders of the new Michael age to the achievements of significant authors who were influenced by anthroposophy. This movement may properly be called the New Age Movement in literature. It is still in the ascending arc of its development, and its greatest works are yet to be written.

The Basic Books of Rudolf Steiner

THE MYSTERY DRAMAS AND THE RENEWAL OF THE ARTS

Additional names could be added to the third column of the Wold Literature chart. These authors faced a difficulty similar to that which Thoreau, Melville, and Dickinson endured with their nineteenth century contemporaries. They were largely ignored during their lifetime, and their audience only arose after their deaths. The plays of Albert Steffen and the essays and books of Bernard Lievegoed and Sergei Prokofieff seem to have suffered a similar fate. More to the point, Steiner's contributions to the renewal of the arts also languish today in obscurity. He wrote four plays, oversaw their production, and directed their performances. To assist the actors and actresses, he developed a new art of speaking, which he called speech formation. He also initiated a completely new art form, which he called eurythmy. Steiner viewed his own artistic work as deeply connected with the German cultural stream. His first mystery drama, *The Portal of Initiation*, was inspired by his long study of Goethe's "The Fairy Tale of the Green Snake and the Beautiful Lily." He even included a chart in the preface relating Goethe's characters to his own.

CHART IX
World Literature

Genres	Classical Greece	Idealism	Anthroposophia
History (Saturn) Character	Herodotus Thucydides	Wolfram's Parzival	Gandhi and Mandela autobiographies
Philosophy (Jupiter) Worldview	Aristotle	Fichte, Schelling, and Hegel (Idealism)	Nietzsche Steiner
Dramas (Mars) Plot	Aeschylus Sophocles Euripides	Shakespeare Moliere Schiller	Ibsen Chekhov Shaw
Epics (Sun) Theme	Homer	Goethe's Faust	Dostoyevsky Clemens Thornton Wilder
Poetry (Venus) Setting	Pindar Sappho	Wordsworth, Keats, and Shelley (Romanticism)	Yeats T.S. Eliot Frost
Essays (Mercury) Thoughts	Plato	Emerson Thoreau (Transcendentalism)	Dr. M.L. King, Jr. sermons
Myths (Moon) Symbol	Hesiod Aesop	Grimm's folk tales	Tolstoy C.S. Lewis J.R.R. Tolkien

Steiner's *Four Mystery Dramas* (CW 14) was a serious attempt to renew the ancient mysteries in a form appropriate to the present day. What the tragic poets had brought to the temple of Dionysos in Athens, Steiner produced in the festival hall in Munich. The scenery was an effort to picture the elemental world and other regions of the soul and spirit worlds, not in symbolic and allegorical manner, but in a spiritually accurate way using physical materials and colors. Each summer from 1910 to 1913, the troop performed a new play. Members of the Anthroposophical Society—amateur actors, but dedicated to the project, and assisted by other members who took on the manifold tasks of a stage production—brought life to a modern form of the lesser mysteries of Greece through public performances. Students of the *Four Mystery Dramas* tend to view *The Portal of Initiation* as a revelation of the soul ordeals of Johannes; *The Soul's Probation* as the trials of Capesius; *The Guardian of the Threshold* as the trials of Maria; and *The Soul's Awakening* as unveiling the trials of Strader. Rudolf Steiner commented that the *Four Mystery Dramas* contain all of anthroposophy.[12] In this respect they constitute a basic book.

THE SECOND PERIOD: 1909 - 1916

The difficulty in understanding Steiner's plays often lies in the interdependence and interrelationships of the characters. His prefaces to the last two plays address this question directly by arranging the characters into four different groups. Steiner gave a lecture cycle after the production of the final play, in which he presented a more complete answer. In *Human and Cosmic Thought* (CW 151), he discussed the clockwise movement of the human being through the twelve signs of the zodiac (i.e., the twelve worldviews) in each successive incarnation. This framework elucidates the circle of twelve characters that appears in each play. In the first play, a group of twelve characters in the present day comes on stage together in the last scene, which takes place in the Sun Temple. In the second play, the same group of twelve is shown at a castle in Austria in scenes six through nine, this time appearing as they were in their fourteenth century incarnations. In the third play, the twelve characters again join together in the final scene, this time in the earthly realm in a Rosicrucian temple. In the last play, the climax in the eighth scene shows the group of twelve taking part in an initiation ceremony in ancient Egypt around the fourteenth century B.C.

THE BASIC BOOKS OF RUDOLF STEINER

A study of Shakespeare's plays, especially his tragedies, reveals similar circles of twelve characters. Steiner pointed out that the tragedy of *Hamlet* is about a later incarnation of the circle that took part in the Trojan War, and that Hamlet is the reincarnated Hector. From the scene in which Hamlet requests the First Player to recite the tale of the death of King Priam, the attentive student can glean the identities of the earlier incarnations of five other characters in *Hamlet*. Shakespeare suggested in *Antony and Cleopatra* that Antony was a later incarnation of Hercules. A study of the *Argonautica* of Apollonius reveals another circle of twelve, whom the Greeks referred to as the great Heroes, as the previous incarnations of the leaders of the Roman Empire who are portrayed in Shakespeare's plays.

The success of the summer festivals in Munich led to the formation of the Johannes Building Association in order to raise money for a permanent home for the plays. The Anthroposophical Society was founded following the performance of the third mystery drama in 1912. After the performance of the fourth play, Steiner decided upon a permanent location for the home of the new Society. In Dornach, Switzerland, on September 20, 1913, Steiner laid the

The Second Period: 1909 - 1916

foundation stone, composed of two interpenetrating pentagondodecahedrons, under the spot where the speaker's dais would stand. The dais stood in front of the stage where the Mystery Dramas, Goethe's *Faust*, and Albert Steffen's plays would be performed. Steiner, who was also the architect, designed a building with a roof formed by two interpenetrating domes situated on the east-west axis. Schionatulander's mission to unite the East and the West, first pictured in *Parzival* and accomplished in spirit during the first period of the Anthroposophical Movement with the publications of *Knowledge of Higher Worlds* and *Occult Science*, was now realized in physical form through the architecture of the Dornach building. In 1917, thirty-three years after taking up the task of editing Goethe's natural scientific writings, Steiner told the membership that the building most of them referred to as the Johannes Building would now be called the Goetheanum.

The fifth mystery drama, scheduled for August of 1914, could not be written or produced because of the onset of World War I, yet work on the Goetheanum proceeded. Artists, sculptors, and architects from all around the world had gathered in Dornach in late 1913 to contribute to the renewal of the mysteries begun by Steiner's dramas. Just as the Greek tragedies had been performed in a temple with sacred statues and painted walls and masks, so were the new Mystery Dramas to be set in exquisite architecture, with intersecting domes covered by Norwegian slate, carved columns with painted planetary seals, a statue of the Representative of Man, and twenty-five-foot high stained glass windows based on Steiner's own sketches. This symphony of the fine arts would harmonize with the poetry, music, and eurythmy of Steiner's plays to create an experience as profound and awe-inspiring as those that the heights of Athenian culture had known. Yet the guns of August delayed the timetable for completing the Goetheanum. The volunteers, once numbering in the hundreds, lost all males of age for military service. The remaining members became a counterpoint to the war raging around them, an oasis of brotherhood, peace, and hope for mankind's future.

The effect of World War I on the spiritual atmosphere of the earth was calamitous. Only Steiner's continued presence, his ability to inspire and uplift, enabled the work on the Goetheanum to proceed. Steiner had to cease other activities, such as those involving the Freemasonic lodge that he had led. His

The Second Period: 1909 - 1916

attempt to enliven and renew Freemasonry was actually brought to a close, not even to be taken up after the cessation of hostilities. In his autobiography, Steiner discussed the reasons for the dissolution of the Lodge and the behavior of certain lodge members who attacked his work. In response to the criticism that he could have known about their betrayal if he had used his occult powers, Steiner agreed. He also pointed out that such use of spiritual faculties is forbidden (i.e., only if a person asks should such spiritual investigation be undertaken), and that he would rather think highly of people and hope for the best than become cynical and distrusting.

A more complete explanation of the reasons for the closing of the Lodge would also have to include what Steiner learned about the actual causes of the war. From the end of 1916 into January of 1917, Steiner gave a cycle of twenty-five lectures on the occult background of the First World War and how it fit into the plans of certain Western secret societies, including some Freemasonic lodges, to achieve world domination. In *The Karma of Untruthfulness* (CW 173-4), Steiner showed in detail how World War I was a manipulated event, and how the "socialist experiment" (i.e. Bolshevism, which had yet to appear on the world stage) was part of it. He believed that knowledge of the truth is the best protection against the misuse of occult powers that these secret societies engage in. The next stage of their plan was to create a materialistic, highly technological culture to trap the souls of young people in order to achieve control over them. Standing in their way was the culture of Idealism and its emphasis on the free individual. The nefarious goal of bringing commercialism, sports, and entertainment together into what later became known as Americanism also faced a newer opposing force: the rise of the sun regency, and the entrance of anthroposophy into the artistic realm and into the cultural sphere as a whole. The attack on Germany was meant to reduce German culture to rubble. What World War I began, Adolf Hitler would complete, and Americanism would reap the reward.

Steiner explained the dangers that Americanism would pose to modern human beings. Without knowledge of the real purpose of Americanism, the threat of modern media and what Steiner called "Ahriman's offer of an alternative electronic reality"—a virtual world of seeming clairvoyance—would go unnoticed. In simplest terms, Americanism acts to create a kind of poison in the human body, which

The Second Period: 1909 - 1916

works on the soul to produce outbursts of rage against other human beings, undergird by a vehement hatred of human culture and any form of education that leads to its appreciation. The goal of Americanism is to deny freedom to the human soul, and in doing so to make the attainment of the high purpose of this modern age an impossibility. Steiner did not directly identify himself or the Anthroposophical Society as the primary targets of the Western secret societies. Yet without knowledge of how Steiner exposed their plans, the attacks on Steiner and the Society that occurred in the third period of the Anthroposophical Movement would not make sense or appear in their proper context. Anthroposophy promotes education towards freedom and attempts to inspire a culture worthy of free human beings.

Alongside his cultural endeavors in the second period of anthroposophy's development, Steiner was able to meet the wishes of those members who wanted to deepen their understanding of religion, especially of the Bible. He lectured on *Genesis* (CW 122) and *Matthew* (CW 123) in 1910, and on *Mark* (CW 139) in 1912, completing a series of cycles on Genesis, the four Gospels, and Revelations. In 1913, after laying the Foundation Stone for the

Goetheanum, he gave a lecture cycle entitled *The Fifth Gospel* (CW 148). He told the story of the incarnation of Zarathustra, who was visited by the three wise men—the Magi—and grew up to experience the downfall of the mysteries of antiquity. In the chart at the end of Part II he is called the Master Jesus, and can be viewed as the human leader of the Southern mystery stream. Steiner was active in that stream as well as the other three; he had entered the mystery center at Ephesus during his incarnation as the pre-Socratic philosopher, Cratylus. In addition to other religious and Biblical topics, Steiner also lectured on the life between death and rebirth and how to remain in contact with those who had crossed over the threshold. In a war in which over eight million soldiers died, with perhaps over twice that number of civilians killed, and in which the number of casualties reached thirty-seven million, nearly everyone had experienced the loss of a loved one or friend.[13]

When the split with the Theosophical Society finally occurred in 1912, Steiner continued to work with the members of the Esoteric School, as he had with the members of the German Section. Yet just as the Freemasonic lodge closed because of World War I, so too the Esoteric School. The difference was that

The Second Period: 1909 - 1916

Steiner would again resume his work with individual students of the Esoteric School after Armistice Day. Steiner had made clear to Annie Besant that he would develop the ritual-knowledge work and esoteric lessons independently. He later resumed giving esoteric lessons from 1920 to 1923 (see CW 266) and took new approaches to ritual-knowledge work in the same years (see CW 265).

Chart X summarizes the important activities and written works of the second period of the Anthroposophical Movement. It is a continuation of chart VIII and again uses the idea of the four mystery streams of Europe from the work of Bernard Lievegoed.

CHART X

The Renewal of the Arts and the Second Period of the Anthroposophical Movement
(1909 — 1916)

STEINER

NORTHERN STREAM

ARISTOTLE

The Calendar of the Soul
(CW 40) — 1912

Founding the
Anthroposophical Society
1912

The Riddles of Philosophy
(CW 18) — 1914

Guiding the First Section of the
Esoteric School
(until WWI)

ROSENKREUTZ

WESTERN STREAM

AQUINAS

*Threshold of the
Spiritual World*
(CW 17) — 1913

Guiding a
Freemasonic Lodge
(until WWI)

PARZIVAL

EASTERN STREAM

SCHIONATULANDER

Way to Self-Knowledge
(CW 16) — 1912

Mystery Dramas
(CW 14) — 1910-1913

Building the Goetheanum
(Foundation Stone — 1913)

MASTER JESUS

SOUTHERN STREAM

CRATYLUS

*Spiritual Guidance of Man
and Humanity*
(CW 15) — 1911

Lectures on the Bible
(CW 122-3, 139)

The Fifth Gospel
(CW 148) — 1913

Part III:
THE SOCIAL INITIATIVES AND THE THIRD PERIOD OF THE ANTHROPOSOPHICAL MOVEMENT (1916-1923) AND THE FOUNDING OF THE GENERAL ANTHROPOSOPHICAL SOCIETY (1923-1925)

THE THREEFOLD SOCIAL ORDER AND THE OPPORTUNITY FOR SOCIAL RENEWAL

Work on the Goetheanum continued throughout the war years. Steiner envisioned the home of the Anthroposophical Society as a cultural center for the renewal of the arts. Before Steiner named it the Goetheanum, it was often called the Johannes Building, or the House of the Word. This union of the Anthroposophical Society and its cultural mission was clearly expressed at the time of its founding in 1912. Thirty-three years after the dawn of the new sun regency in 1879 and the accompanying creation of four masterpieces of world literature, the Anthroposophical Society was founded.

Steiner viewed the Mystery Dramas, and *The Portal of Initiation* in particular, as the fruit of his intense study of Goethe's fairy tale. Undertaken right before his visit to Budapest in 1889, his meditations on "The Fairy Tale of the Green Snake and the Beautiful Lily" constituted the conclusion of the first period of his life. He joined the Goethe Archives in Weimar the following year. The climax of Goethe's tale was the gradual rising from subterranean depths of the mystery temple of the four kings. Steiner renewed the fairy tale through the performances of the four Mystery Dramas in Munich from 1910 to 1913. He next transformed it into the mystery temple itself through the magnificence of the Goetheanum. By 1922, the painted dome, carved columns, stained glass windows, and stage were finished. All that remained was the completion and installation of the statue of the Representative of Man. Thirty-three years after taking up the study of Goethe's tale, Steiner was ready to bring the Mystery Dramas to the Goetheanum stage.

The arson that turned this height of architecture and the arts into a smoldering ruin occurred on the final day of 1922. Set by a Nazi who perished in the

The Third Period: 1916 - 1923

blaze that he had ignited, the fire exposed the opponents of Idealism whose hatred inflamed not only the political sphere but the religious and economic realms as well. Steiner said that it revealed the jealousy of man. In truth, the same human beings who helped push the nations into the war and used World War I as a smokescreen to establish Bolshevism now tried to halt humanity's advance towards freedom by directly attacking the society that bore the name of the ruler of the sun regency in an attempt to prevent the growth of the Anthroposophical Movement.

The following year, Rudolf Steiner led the Anthroposophical Society to actively take up the task of building a second Goetheanum, but this time with concrete and steel, not wood. A new founding was not necessary. Steiner assured members that the foundation, which had remained in place, would continue in its service to the second building. The statue of the Representative of Man alone survived. It stands today in the rebuilt Goetheanum as a testament to Steiner's genius in yet another realm—that of sculpture.

The third period of the Anthroposophical Movement "demanded that what had been achieved through knowledge and had become visible through art should now become deed in the sphere of social unity."[1] During the Great War, Steiner had discovered a practical way to engage with the problems that had led to war. Asked by two important leaders, one from Bavaria and the other from Austria, for advice about a correct solution to the social problems besetting Europe, Steiner travelled to Berlin to meet with them. On July 17, 1917, less than a week after the meeting, he presented them with what they had requested—memoranda of his conversations with them, which they could then share with other world leaders. The memoranda were basically an outline for what Steiner would publish after the war in 1919 as *The Threefold Social Order* (CW 23).

While the plan itself was eminently down-to-earth and practical, implementing it required that a large number of people—a majority—agree with and understand its central concepts. Only a large-scale educational initiative could hope to bring about such a change in public opinion. Steiner himself came forth to give lectures in large halls as well as in factories. He even gave courses to members on the art of lecturing in order to increase the number of lecturers. With the release of *The Threefold Social Order* in April, the accessibility of Steiner's ideas expanded immensely. Over eighty thousand copies sold in the

The Third Period: 1916 - 1923

first year. Yet the window for change, which had opened following the armistice, soon began to close. Though at first successful, the economic venture formed to support Steiner's initiative, *Der Kommende Tag*, also experienced difficulties. By the middle of 1922, Steiner could no longer lecture in public for fear of assassination, and the businesses brought together under *Der Kommende Tag*—including various industrial and agricultural enterprises, a medical clinic and Weleda, and a publishing house and research laboratory—experienced difficulties, and some failed.[2] The Goetheanum burned at the close of 1922. The opponents appeared victorious.

In the summer of 1922, Steiner gave a lecture cycle entitled *World Economy* (CW 340) to a group of economics students at Dornach who had requested it. Over the course of fourteen days, Steiner dealt directly with the problem of the mistaken concepts of modern national economics in detail. More importantly, the lectures developed the correct economic ideas and showed how they pointed to realities, not abstractions. While a discussion of the basic books of Rudolf Steiner is not an appropriate place to enter into these economic ideas, one of them is crucial for grasping the solution that Steiner believed was within mankind's reach. The title of the lecture course, properly understood, states that solution. It also points towards the reason that modern economics is unable to find a solution. While certain dark forces brought on the war for their own selfish purposes, Steiner believed that in actuality they only accelerated what was fated to occur. The rest of the twentieth century and especially the events in the second decade of the twenty-first century show that interweaving production and distribution of goods around the globe as a method for producing a world economy tends to a return of the old economic ideas, embraces isolationism and tariffs, and in fact destroys the world economy by encouraging white nationalism and a nationalist economics that puts the strongest individual private economy back in charge.

THE SOCIAL INITIATIVES FOUNDED ON THE IMPULSE OF FREEDOM

Within the first six months following the armistice, the window of opportunity closed, and the eventual collapse of the endeavor to move from a unitary state to a threefold society became apparent. Steiner looked to the field of education to provide the next best hope for a positive future for free human

The Third Period: 1916 - 1923

beings. In the fall of 1919, Emil Molt's request for help founding a school to educate the children of the workers in his Waldorf-Astoria cigarette factory led to the first Waldorf School in Stuttgart, Germany. Molt's generosity enabled the school to thrive. Chosen and trained by Steiner, the teachers themselves carried the pedagogical responsibilities of the school. Through a series of lectures, discussions, and practical advice, Steiner prepared them for this task. These three seminal works—*The Study of Man, Discussions with Teachers*, and *Practical Advice for Teachers* (CW 293-295)—are still used today in Waldorf teacher training institutes. Many of the original teachers trained by Steiner helped prepare the next generation of teachers to carry the Waldorf School movement into the future.

Steiner's insight into the four temperaments of childhood and the adolescent soul qualities helped teachers deepen their understanding of their pupils. Steiner's gift of the secrets belonging to each year of the seven-year cycles was of even greater assistance in forming the curriculum to meet the talents of each individual child. The same basic truth persisted throughout: the teacher's own willingness to take up the path of self-development determines whether or not the student will accept a fairy tale or a masterpiece of world literature, an addition fact or a eurythmy form, into his or her soul as a seed that will blossom forth years later as a free deed. If the teacher cannot exemplify freedom in his or her own life, the hope that children can attain this ideal is somewhat naïve. The hallmark of Waldorf education is the teachers, themselves inspired to work out of anthroposophical sources and create a lesson plan or a block all their own. Copying what Steiner said to do or what other Waldorf teachers have found to be successful may be better than what for-profit charter schools offer, or even superior to the state-mandated testing in the public schools, but it cannot rise to the true ideal of education unless the teachers know that their true calling is to inspire. The reason that Steiner spent such a great deal of time at the first Waldorf School was similar to why he devoted himself to the first Goetheanum so completely during the war years: he wanted to uplift and free the higher self of those engaged in the art of teaching so that the teachers might enter upon a path appropriate to the present cultural age.

In the summer of 1921, Guenther Wachsmuth created a research laboratory in the basement of the

The Third Period: 1916 - 1923

"Glass House," the building where the Goetheanum windows were being engraved. Joined by Ehrenfried Pfeiffer, he began conducting scientific experiments on the body of formative forces, also called the life ether. With Steiner's guidance, they began systematizing the theory of the formative forces and conducting experiments to render visible the world of forces active in living organisms. Out of this small, under-equipped Dornach research lab came the preparations for the new biological-dynamic methods in agriculture that Steiner would introduce to the world.[3]

Wachsmuth identified the following year, 1922, as the time of the actual birth of the Biodynamic agriculture movement. After working for a year in the Glass House, Guenther and Ehrenfried went to Steiner to ask for advice on how to make the results of their research practical in the field of agriculture. Steiner obliged and recommended preparing substances in different seasons of the year and at different times of the day, exposing them to the elements in various ways, and even enclosing them in cows horns. He then suggested the farmer should then dilute the preparations, which contained highly concentrated forces, so that they could be spread across the arable fields. These methods and much more went into the first B-D preparations. Being scientists, Guenther and Ehrenfried asked innumerable questions and took copious notes. They were awe-struck when Steiner answered their queries immediately and precisely. Unfortunately, they did not record the exact spot where they had buried the cow horns that fall. The next spring, upon Steiner's visit to the field, the scientists almost came up empty-handed; yet good fortune intervened, allowing Steiner to demonstrate how to add the contents of the horns to pitchers of water and mix them properly.[4]

In 1924, Steiner spoke to a group of farmers at the request of Count Keyserlingk. The Agricultural Course (CW 327), as it has come to be known, served much the same purpose as the pedagogical courses (CW 293-295) of 1919. Steiner taught that farmers need to become aware of the cosmic forces that stream down from the starry heavens and the planetary spheres in order to prepare the soil for healthful plant growth and heal the dying earth, just as teachers need to acknowledge the soul-spirit being of the child and assist it incarnating into his or her physical body by forming the subject knowledge of the class lessons into seed-like imaginations that can enter the child's soul, grow, and mature into living thoughts in adulthood.

The Third Period: 1916 - 1923

Neither genetically modified seeds grown with the help of artificial fertilizers and pesticides, nor abstractions and intellectual concepts parroted back on tests, can promote healthful living. The 1924 agriculture conference led to the creation of what Steiner called the "Research Ring." The new agricultural initiative was able to grow and expand around the globe because the unity of the pioneer farmers and the spiritual scientific researchers held firm. Their successes and failures helped clarify the fundamental ideas that Steiner had laid out. Their further experiments led to public conferences and, finally, to results that could speak for themselves.[5]

Anthroposophical medicine was the third major initiative that Steiner began in the third seven-year period of the Anthroposophical Movement. It plays a significant role in modern society nearly a century after its founding. Steiner gave the first medical course in the spring of 1920 as a cycle of twenty lectures to doctors and medical students, later published under the title *Spiritual Science and Medicine* (CW 312). As he opened up new perspectives in the fields of anatomy, physiology, pathology, and therapy, Steiner emphasized that the actual practice of medicine must be left to the doctor. A second course for doctors was given a year later and published as *Spiritual Scientific Points of View in Therapy* (CW 313).

Research on anthroposophical remedies began alongside the research on Biodynamic preparations in the Dornach research lab in 1920. Both Wachsmuth and Pfeiffer received suggestions and prescriptions for medical remedies from Steiner. Dr. Ludwig Noll joined them during the first medical course and helped immensely. The lab was later incorporated into the Weleda Corporation, which is still an important producer of remedies for anthroposophical doctors down to the present day. The founding of the Clinical-Therapeutic Institute by Dr. Ita Wegman in Arlesheim, Switzerland, accomplished in the presence of Steiner, provided the anthroposophical medical movement with an important new impulse. As early as 1905, upon Steiner's advice, Dr. Wegman had gone to Switzerland, completed her medical studies in Zurich, and established a small private clinic there. By June of 1921, she had become an active collaborator with Steiner; in October of the following year, she worked with him to help deliver the third course for doctors.

In 1922, Steiner met with a small group of medical students who asked him for advice about the

The Third Period: 1916 - 1923

humanizing of medicine. It was not until early 1924 that he could give them a proper reply and reveal the source of true medical ethics—the medical attitude of mind. He entitled his course for young physicians *Ethics in the Study and Practice of Medicine*. Through many other lecture cycles, Steiner helped expand the healing arts into related fields, including curative pedagogy, color therapy, and curative eurythmy. Most important for the entire medical movement, Steiner completed *Essentials for Expansion of the Art of Healing according to Spiritual Scientific Insights* (CWS 27) in 1924. He wrote this comprehensive work in collaboration with Dr. Wegman. Just as teachers need to become like farmers if their efforts in planting the seeds of knowledge are to bear fruit, so must doctors become like farmers who seek to heal the earth, if they seek to successfully set free the forces of healing within the human soul and restore the health of their patients.

The three initiatives discussed so far—Waldorf education, Biodynamic agriculture, and anthroposophical medicine—all suffer from a common misunderstanding. The practitioner of any of these disciplines must remember that Steiner's spiritual and intellectual development was consistent. One of its high points came in 1894 at the age of thirty-three with the publication of *The Philosophy of Freedom*. Steiner did not abandon his belief in this high ideal and later expect teachers, farmers, and doctors simply to follow his advice. Rather, he believed that the insights that he provided about the growing child, the healing of the earth, and the healing of the human being might inspire others. Such inspiration, freely taken in, can harmonize with the free deeds a person has already undertaken. Those individuals who believe that Steiner's ideas can serve as a substitute for the active thinking of a free human being suffer from a grave misunderstanding that cannot be corrected by pointing out the error with words.

Another kind of confusion surrounds the fourth initiative that Steiner provided an impulse for—the Movement for Religious Renewal. Many people view anthroposophy itself as a religion. This narrative attempted to dispel that notion in the discussion of *Christianity as Mystical Fact*. Anthroposophy is a path of knowledge, and its goal is to uncover the deeper truths of all religions. Steiner lectured on Buddhism, Hinduism, and other Eastern religions as well as those of the West. The membership of the Anthroposophical Society included practicing members of all the

The Third Period: 1916 - 1923

world's religions. Steiner referred to anthroposophy as "spiritual science," but of course the misunderstanding persisted. To be sure, some members of the Society were not members of any church, and many of these did indeed find their religious needs met by the study of anthroposophy. Two key members of the Society talked to Steiner about this very fact. Guenther Wachsmuth, member of the first executive council of the Anthroposophical Society in 1924, and Friedrich Rittelmeyer, the future leader of the Christian Community, in 1925. The two men talked with each other and agreed that the path of anthroposophy, despite its complete absence of church ritual, could lead to the same goal espoused by religion.

In June of 1921, Steiner undertook preparatory work with eighteen young men interested in developing a movement for religious renewal by delivering the five lectures of the first theology course (CW 342). Steiner explained that he was not lecturing on theology or the activity of the spiritual hierarchies in the earthly realm. Rather, he was introducing the young men to a longer course of lectures that he would give in Dornach at Michaelmas as an essential advance toward the founding of the "Christian Community." In September of 1921, a group of over a hundred people assembled to hear the second Theology course (CW 343), which consisted of fifteen morning lectures followed by afternoon discussions about a new kind of religious teaching as well as new rituals.[6]

The following Michaelmas, Steiner delivered a third course for theologians (CW 344) for around forty-five participants. Again, the element of individual freedom was decisive, as only those church leaders and seminary students returned who wanted to participate freely in a new kind of religious movement. The essential part of these fourteen gatherings was not just the content of the lectures, but the substance of a new ritual that Steiner bestowed upon these persons. Earlier in his life, Steiner had freely and independently developed ritual knowledge for the Esoteric School and the Freemasonic lodge in accord with actual spiritual experiences that occur as the soul enters the higher worlds. Now Steiner accomplished a similar deed for the Christian path, which he had first outlined in his basic book of 1902, *Christianity as Mystical Fact*. He founded the Christian Community through the inauguration of the cultic liturgy and the consecration of the priests. Now a clear distinction between the Anthroposophical Society and religion could be drawn. For those

The Third Period: 1916 - 1923

anthroposophists interested in participating in a religious group inspired by anthroposophical insights, there is the Christian Community of the Movement for Religious Renewal. For all other members, there is the choice of any of other religion or no religion at all.

STEINER'S CORE MISSION AND THE FOUNDING OF THE GENERAL ANTHROPOSOPHICAL SOCIETY

The burning of the Goetheanum at the end of 1922, though a great disaster, could not touch the heart of the Anthroposophical Movement—the spiritual being of Anthroposophia. Yet it did provoke a kind of self-examination, as the third period of the movement drew to a close. Momentous changes had signaled the beginning of both the second and the third period. They suggested that an equally momentous transformation would be forthcoming. Steiner began discussions amongst the leading members in an attempt to identify the mistakes that had occurred and the changes that might be made in the Society itself to correct them. Gradually the majority of members joined in. Steiner more clearly expressed his view of the problem by speaking of the three periods of the Anthroposophical Movement—the same three periods that Wachsmuth would later use in his biography of Steiner. Steiner noted that the outward thrust of the anthroposophical social initiatives had provoked opposition, but also had gained widespread support and had spread anthroposophical ideas throughout society. A more basic problem—one that had to be addressed—was that it took up the members' time and energy and weakened the group life of the Anthroposophical Society. A contradictory situation had arisen in which the increased vitality and strength of the initiatives corresponded to a weakened and ineffectual Anthroposophical Society. Were this situation to continue, the source and wellspring of the anthroposophical ventures would wither and dry up, and the social initiatives would themselves become bureaucratic and gradually perish.

The spiritual being of Anthroposophia—the archangel of the sun whose regency began in 1879—did not need protection from the adversarial forces that had burned the Goetheanum. Rather, it was the Anthroposophical Society—which had sought to develop a central element for anthroposophical life through study groups and artistic festivals—that required the protection provided by the active support of a dedicated membership. Steiner spoke of

The Third Period: 1916 - 1923

how he must turn his full attention to this solemn duty. He concluded that only a new founding of the Anthroposophical Society could solve the dilemma that it had fallen into. This founding had to make possible for the individual members the same commitment that Steiner saw himself making. In the first instance, it required Steiner to dismount his high horse, as it were, and no longer serve as the spirit guide of the movement,—but become a member like any other. Secondly, it required the creation of a path for members to maintain their connection with the society whatever the demands of the anthroposophical initiatives or their own life situations might prove to be. An individual, seemingly alone and overwhelmed, would yet be able to participate in building an anthroposophical community. *The Christmas Conference for the Founding of the General Anthroposophical Society* (CW 260) accomplished this mighty task. It enabled Rudolf Steiner to unite with the Society and become its executive leader, rather than its spiritual leader. The Foundation Stone Meditation provided a pathway for members to join with him, gain new insights into how to work with fellow anthroposophists, and build a spiritual Goetheanum.

THE BASIC BOOKS OF RUDOLF STEINER

Following the Christmas Conference, Rudolf Steiner began writing what he called "the leading thoughts," which were published weekly in the *Goetheanum Newsletter*. Far more than an advanced course, *Anthroposophical Leading Thoughts* (CW 26) served much like the creation of a new spiritual language appropriate to bring the mysteries of the heavenly realms into the purview of mortal men and women. Carl Unger called the new vocabulary that Steiner had developed for this task "the language of the consciousness soul." Unger's book by the same name remains his greatest gift to anthroposophy. Guiding anthroposophical study groups for over two decades prepared Unger to take on the seemingly impossible task of exploring and explaining the *Leading Thoughts*. What Steiner previously had hoped to plant in the heart of individual members as a meditation, he now unfolded for their active thinking as pure thoughts. Unger not only followed Steiner's line of thinking, he elucidated it.

During the founding of the General Anthroposophical Society, Rudolf Steiner also reconstituted the Esoteric School as the School of Spiritual Science. He led what he now called the Michael School for nine months and was able to establish the First Class and

The Third Period: 1916 - 1923

the Sections. He did not live long enough to establish the Second and Third Classes. When the general copyright for Rudolf Steiner's work ran out in 1995, the leadership of the School of Spiritual Science decided to publish the contents of the First Class lessons. The First Class mantrams (CW 270) are thus available, and the attempt to maintain their secrecy has ended. Considering that much of what Steiner wrote about and lectured on had been esoteric knowledge intentionally kept hidden from the common man for millennia, the open publication of these mantrams aligns perfectly with Steiner's fundamental goal in this age of freedom. The First Class mantrams show what actually constitutes the modern path of initiation. The mantrams form the third aspect of the anthroposophical path, which entered the feeling realm as the Foundation Stone Meditation and then the thinking realm as the *Leading Thoughts*. The soul's journey continues in the realm of willing, where the First Class mantrams become genuine spiritual experiences.

Long after Steiner's death, an anthroposophist stepped forward to accomplish for the First Class mantrams what Carl Unger, the O'Neils, and Rudolf Grosse had done for the basic books, and what Carl

Unger and Karl Konig had done for the advanced courses—an accomplishment perhaps as awe-inspiring as the mantrams themselves. Sergei Prokofieff's *The First Class of the Michael School and Its Christological Foundation* laid the groundwork for his final book about the First Class mantrams and the General Anthroposophical Society. The assistance that Prokofieff brought to those who wished to tread the Michael path in the present day is fitting testimony to the devotion that he displayed towards the trailblazer of this path.

Rudolf Steiner accomplished so much by writing the basic books, producing the Mystery Dramas, completing the many artistic projects that accompanied them, and inspiring major social initiatives, that it is difficult to relate them to one another and form a proper estimate of their relative importance. One reason to include the charts that appear at the end of each of the three parts of this book is to assist in such a valuation. Steiner himself had opinions about his accomplishments, and one view that he held is particularly important for understanding the group of eighty lectures that he gave in 1924 on the subject of *Karmic Relationships* (CW 235-240). Much of what we do in life is to earn a living and to help other people, but Steiner believed, as did Emerson, that each of us brings a specific mission to earth with us that only we can accomplish, and that would remain undone were we to neglect it. For Emerson, this true purpose was to lecture on the "Natural History of the Intellect." For Steiner, it was to lecture on Karma and Reincarnation. His mission would have remained unfulfilled had he not given that cycle of eighty lectures. Steiner believed that without the knowledge of the laws of destiny and of reincarnation, modern human beings would lack what they need most to live properly in this earthly realm.

I have to assume that many anthroposophists have studied these lectures, but I have not read any research that takes them up in depth. The study of *Karmic Relationships* can bear fruit in the next life by developing a faculty for gaining insight into the past lives of people whom one might meet in the future. An earlier discussion of Konig's *Commentary on The Calendar of the Soul* mentioned the development of a faculty of foreseeing future events. The ability to see past lives is similar, but it allows one to comprehend the opposite stream of time. Like any talent, it arises as the result of practice in a past life; e.g., to possess math talent in a future life, it is necessary to study math and to make use of it in the present life. Steiner especially wished to bestow on his contemporaries and all of mankind a course of study suited to the development of the talent for perceiving past lives. He saw it as the firm basis on which a community could be built, and the answer to the question of how to lead a better life.

One law of karma that Steiner had to observe concerned the year in which he could publicly reveal himself to be an initiate. Having waited until the age of forty before he founded the German section of the Theosophical Society and began to publish the basic books of anthroposophy, Steiner was then required to observe another law. He had to give an account of his life—to write an autobiography—so that people would know what events, people, and books had influenced him. This was necessary so that his life would become an open book, as it were, and people could judge for themselves whether his spiritual and intellectual development was truly consistent. In the present age of freedom, people have the right and obligation to know the facts about the lives of those who would take on the role of being a spiritual leader. Some of the greatest autobiographies of the twentieth century—Gandhi's *The Story of my Experiments with*

The Third Period: 1916 - 1923

Truth, The Autobiography of Malcolm X, and Mandela's *Long Walk to Freedom*—have been written to meet this basic need.

Rudolf Steiner's *The Course of My Life* was written as weekly installments that appeared in *The Goetheanum Newsletter* in the same fashion as *Anthroposophical Leading Thoughts*. The first chapter came out at the end of the third period of the Anthroposophical Movement, and the seventieth chapter appeared five days after his death. Werner Glas (mentioned previously in the discussion of *The Riddles of Philosophy*) maintained that Steiner's autobiography was also a basic book—the seventh one. It was certainly written for the general public, and it required no special knowledge of anthroposophy to be understood. Steiner went out of his way to explain how each further step on his path to knowledge of the spirit came about, and what the difficulties were that he experienced in making each advance. The idea that these steps represented a path of initiation is relevant only in retrospect—Steiner himself did not discuss his own biography in such terms—and important only insofar as we consider the question of whether or not *The Course of My Life* is a basic book and presents a full path to the higher worlds. Many anthroposophists have written studies about this book, one of the deepest being Prokofieff's *Rudolf Steiner and the Founding of the New Mysteries.*

A chart showing Steiner's activities during the third period of the Anthroposophical Movement, as well as the year that followed the founding of the General Anthroposophical Society and Steiner's union with it, brings this overview of the basic books of Rudolf Steiner to a close.

CHART XI

*The Social Initiatives and the Third Period of the
Anthroposophical Movement (1916 — 1923)
The Founding of the General Anthroposophical Society (1923-25)*

STEINER

| NORTHERN STREAM |

ARISTOTLE

Founding of the first
Waldorf School
(CW 293-5) — 1919

Christmas Conference
Founding the General
Anthroposophical Society
(CW 260) — 1923/24

*Anthroposophical Leading
Thoughts*
(CW 36) — 1924-25

ROSENKREUTZ   **PARZIVAL**

| WESTERN STREAM | | EASTERN STREAM |

AQUINAS   *SCHIONATULANDER*

Threefold Social Order   Building the
(CW 23) — 1919   Goetheanum
                                     (Through 1922)
Biodynamic agriculture
(CW 327)   First Class of the
                                 Michael School
Anthroposophical   (CW 270) — 1924
medicine
(CW 27)

Karmic Relationships
(CW 235-240) — 1924

MASTER JESUS

| SOUTHERN STREAM |

CRATYLUS

Founding of the Christian
Community
(CW 269) — 1922

The Course of My Life
(CW 28) — 1924-25

APPENDIX

THE FOUNDATION STONE MEDITATION

By Rudolf Steiner
A new translation into the American Plain Style by Rick Spaulding

Soul of Man!
You live in the limbs,
Which bear you through the spatial world
Into the spirit ocean:
Practice spirit-recalling
In depths of soul,
Where in the sublime strength of world-creative might
Your own I
Comes alive
Within God's I,
And you shall truly *live*
In the spiritual world of Man.

For the Father Spirit in the heights holds sway
O'er the depths of the world, creating life.
Spirits of Strength
(Seraphim, Cherubim, Thrones)
Let ring forth from the heights
What echoes back from the depths,
Which speaks:
Out of the Godhead mankind is created.

The nature spirits in the east, west, north,
       and south hear it,—
May human beings hear it.

Soul of Man!
You live in the beat of the heart and the breath of lungs,
Which leads you through the rhythms of time
Into the core of your own soul's feeling:
Practice spirit-meditating
In equanimity of soul,
Where the ever-surging, world-historic deeds
Unite
Your own I
With the world-I,
And you shall truly *feel*
In the soul activity of Man.

For the Will of Christ in the encircling spheres holds sway
O'er the rhythms of the world, shedding grace upon souls.
Spirits of Light
(Kyriotetes, Dynamis, Exusiai)
Let be enkindled in the East
What forms in the West,
Which speaks:
In Christ death becomes life.

The nature spirits in the east, west, north,
       and south hear it,—
May human beings hear it.

Soul of Man!
You live in the resting head,
Which unveils to you the cosmic thoughts
From the wellsprings of eternity:
Practice spirit-envisioning
In stillness of thought,
Where the eternal aims of gods
Bestow the spiritual world's light
On your own I
For freedom of the will,
And you shall truly *think*
In the spiritual wellsprings of Man.

For the Spirit's cosmic thoughts hold sway
O'er the spiritual world, invoking light.
Spirits of Soul
(Archai, Archangeloi, Angeloi)
Let be entreated in the depths
What shall be answered from the heights,
Which speaks:
In the cosmic thoughts of the Spirit the soul awakes.

The nature spirits in the east, west, north,
       and south hear it,—
May human beings hear it.

At the turning point of time
The Spirit Light of the world stepped
Into the stream of earthly life;
Dark night's reign
Ended;
Day-radiant light
Shone forth from human souls;
Light,
That warmed
Poor shepherd's hearts;
Light,
That enlightened
Wise kings' heads.

Light divine,
Christ-sun,
Warm our hearts,
Enlighten our heads,
That what we
Shelter in our hearts,
What we
Direct from our heads
      with singleness of purpose,
May become good.

Endnotes

Part I: The Basic Books

1. *Knowledge of the Higher Worlds and Its Attainment* by Rudolf Steiner (Hudson, New York: Anthroposophic Press, 1947), p.1.
2. *Notes on Theosophy* by Carl Unger (London: St. George Publications, 1982)
3. *Guidance in Esoteric Training* by Rudolf Steiner (London: Rudolf Steiner Press, 1972), p.13.
4. *The Life and Works of Rudolf Steiner* by Guenther Wachsmuth (Blauvelt, New York: Garner Communications, 1989), pp.62–63.
5. "An Autobiographical Sketch" by Rudolf Steiner in *The Essential Steiner*, Robert McDermott, ed. (New York, Harper and Row, 1984), pp.13-15.
6. *Autobiography: Chapters in the Course of My Life* by Rudolf Steiner (Great Barrington, MA: Steiner Books, 2005), p.237.
7. *The Mystery Streams in Europe and the New Mysteries* by Bernard Lievegoed (Hudson, New York: Anthroposophical Press, 1982)
8. *The Battle for the Soul* by Bernard Lievegoed (Gloucester, U.K.: Hawthorne Press, 1994)
9. *Christianity as Mystical Fact* by Rudolf Steiner (Great Barrington, MA: Steiner Books, 2006), p.67.
10. *Autobiography*, op. cit., p.203.

Part II: The Renewal of the Arts

1. *The Spiritual Guidance of the Individual and Humanity* by Rudolf Steiner (Hudson, New York: Anthroposophic Press, 1992), p.1.
2. *Way of Self-Knowledge and The Threshold of the Spiritual World* by Rudolf Steiner (Hudson, New York: Anthroposophic Press, 1999), p.100.
3. Ibid., p.3.

4. *The Life and Work of Rudolf Steiner*, op. cit., p.21.
5. Werner Glas suggested this view of *The Riddles of Philosophy* as a basic book to me in 1985 in connection with an article on the basic books that he wanted written for an introductory pamphlet for new members of the Anthroposophical Society in the Midwest Region.
6. *Autobiography*, op. cit., p.207.
7. *The Living Being "Anthroposophia"* by Rudolf Grosse (Vancouver: Steiner Book Center, 1986), pp.54–56.
8. *The Spiritual Guidance of the Individual and Humanity*, op.cit,. p.vii.
9. Missions of Folk Souls by Rudolf Steiner (New York: Anthroposophic Press, 1929), p.12.
10. Rudolf Steiner preferred to call this adversary by his Persian name—Ahriman or the god of darkness.
11. *The Life and Works of Rudolf Steiner*, op.cit., p.171.
12. Ibid., p.117.
13. "World War I," *Encyclopedia Britannica* (U.S.A.: Encyclopedia Britannica, 1970), vol. 23, p.716.

Part III: The Social Initiatives

1. *The Life and Works of Rudolf Steiner*, op. cit., p.288.
2. Ibid., p.378.
3. Ibid., pp.420–422.
4. Ibid., pp.469–470.
5. Ibid., pp.546–550.
6. Ibid., p.413.

www.ingramcontent.com/pod-product-compliance
Lightning Source LLC
Chambersburg PA
CBHW020656300426
44112CB00007B/408